PRESENTIMENT

ALSO BY BRYANT A. LONEY

Exodus in Confluence

—

A NOVELLA

To Hear the Ocean Sigh

—

A NOVEL

Take Me to the Cat

—

A NOVEL

Sea Breeze Academy

—

A NOVEL

In the College at Night

—

A POETRY COLLECTION

Poems by

BRYANT A. LONEY

☙

LUXAPALILA CREEK
PEPPERNELL
2025

Published by PEPPERNELL
Copyright © 2025 by Bryant A. Loney

All rights reserved. No part of this book may be used or performed without written consent from the author, except for critical articles or reviews. Please do not participate in or promote electronic piracy of copyrighted materials. Please support the author's rights and purchase only authorized editions. Reproduction or use of any part of this book for the training of artificial intelligence technologies or systems is strictly prohibited.

This is a work of creative expression. In honoring both memory and imagination, some names, places, and identifying details have been altered to preserve privacy. Famous figures, where they appear, do so as themselves.

Peppernell is in residence in Fayette, Alabama, by the backing of Luxapalila Creek, a gathering place designed to help writers and artists create and produce. Peppernell books are published and distributed by Verona Booksellers.

Our titles may be purchased in bulk at special quantity discounts for promotional, educational, or business use. Book excerpts can also be created to fit specific needs. For details, write: info@veronabooksellers.com.

ISBN 978-0-9971700-6-1 (trade paperback)
ISBN 978-0-9971700-7-8 (e-book)

Cover and book design by Allison Levens
First Edition: November 2025
10 9 8 7 6 5 4 3 2 1

*To Theodore, cairn terrier,
who cannot read but slept
at my feet while I wrote
most of these.*

If you want to work on your art, work on your life.

—ANTON CHEKHOV

TABLE OF CONTENTS

I: OLD HEART

To the Reader, Welcome Back	3
Where the Giant Creatures Swirl	5
Small Tree at California Gas Station	6
Written Upon Learning Cleopatra Died by Suicide by Having a Cobra Bite Her on the Boob	8
Myth of Myself	10
Watching a Nature Documentary While Your Roommate Has Sex Down the Hall	11
Mr. John James Audubon (1785–1851)	13
A Textual Tour of My *Animal Crossing* Island Based on Memory	15
On This, the One-Hundredth Rejection Letter from Walt Disney Studios, We Reconsider the Magic of Late-Stage Capitalism	17
Roommates, Part Two	19
Oops! Poetry Paywall	21
Nice to See You Again on This Dating App	22
Hydrating Through the Five Stages of Grief	24
Your Life Better	26

II: SEARCHING

Time Travel	29
Summer Elsewhere	30
Middle School Advice, 2008	31
YouTube of Our Years	32
Facebook Messages, 2011	33
Rubies	35
Catfishing	37

Abe	39
"The Dead" by James Joyce	41
The Fault in Our Expectations	42
To Sleep in Spite of Sea; or, The Ghost of Windhaven Beach	44
They Will Know the Truth	46
Heart's Memory	47
Marrying My Girlfriend from High School	49
The Weilanders	51
Two Birds	57
Night Windows	58
Land of Fire and Ice	59
Vented Views	61
How Many Times Have You Been in Love?	62
Rent-a-Friend	64
Rent-a-Friend (Postscript)	66
Things We Don't Talk About	67
Intermission	69
Wine Wednesdays	70
Marie & Michael	72
Feeding Tortilla Chips to Little Birds	73
Night In	75
Daphne, with the Dog, Walks In on Fred Kissing Velma	76
Proposals	77
Reallydrunk (When It's $3.99 Margs and You Have No Self-Control;)	80
A Poem in Which Everyone Finally…	82
We Were Absolutely Wild About Each Other	83
Arctic Monkeys Played Through a Late-Night Radio in the Rain	85
Film Scratches and Dust	86
Firsts	87
The Rich, the Royals & the Rest of Us	88

The Phone Call with Dad Before I Blocked His Number	90
Ramona, California, Fourth of July	91
Beers, Bros, Bungalow	92
The Flavor of Live Fire	103
Hatch Green Chile Lagers	105
Spectrum of Blues	107
When I Think of God	108
The Petco Goth Girl Apologizes Years After	109
My Therapist Asks Why This Obsession	110
Comfort	112
Precious	114
Who Narrates the Narrator	116
Presentiment	117

III: NEW HEART

The Author and the Author at Age Twenty-One Meet Up After the First Poetry Book	127
Chimney Wine	131
These Trails We Travel	132
Dog Park People	134
Lucky Stars	136
How Many Times Have You Been in Love? Again	137
Writing in the Quiet	139
Ready	141
Morning Walks with Theodore	142
Caterpillar in the Grass	144
Friday with Carefree Campers	145
What Are You Afraid Of	147
Graduation Eve	148
One Last Thing	151

NOTES AND ACKNOWLEDGMENTS   153

PRESENTIMENT

I. OLD HEART

TO THE READER, WELCOME BACK

Bryant's been a little depressed! I don't know who
or what I am sometimes. Am I nice, am I mean,
am I self-absorbed? A little rhymes-with-witch?
I stole a fan from a zoo gift shop once when I was seven.
Scoped out the security and everything.
That was twenty years ago. Now I get heartburn
from good cheese fries. Against my will,
I am a dynamic character. Would rather be a frog—
just hop to adjacent lily pads and croak.
Maybe be poisonous, maybe be moisturized.
I lost my writing job, I had to move houses a few times,
I hurt someone I care for deeply, I blew through my savings.
We all have those days, right? Or years.

Then I think of Hayley Reynolds, whose brother I knew
back when we were all kids on the playground.
Her ex-husband texts her, complaining
that she's sending their son Cedar out in capes, he says,
when it would only take a minute to dress him properly.
She says it was fifty degrees when they left the apartment,
and Cedar had a coat on,
and don't you come at me about what our son's wearing
when you haven't been around in years.
How the clothes she sends him out in never make it back.
And Cedar runs hot, anyway—at least, that's what I hope.

What a paragraph can be is only that.
When my parents divorced, I remember cold mornings.

I am alive and will stay that way and, as such,
will be okay at some point, eventually, probably.
I've written new poems; I'll show you soon.
This one's for Cedar. Evening rest.

WHERE THE GIANT CREATURES SWIRL

The underwater scientist in his submarine spaceship
observed you once in the quiet in the coral and fell
in love. How gentle you must be, he said against glass.
Paean to all things oceanic. The catch of a lifetime.
He will name your entire species after you, he will.
Latin with your name and his forever attached as one
within history books and songs sung in school buses.
Statues in shopping malls for your children's children.
When Finsgiving comes each year, they will stand in line
for a cheap-costumed version of you to worship.
Won't you accept these briny bling offerings?
The underwater scientist, he left his wife for you.
He could have chosen any other listless sea creature
for his poetry—and he picked you: poked and prodded
and processed and possessed and proximity to pier to plate
to your petri dish for the other underwater scientists,
who did not leave their wives and are ready for lunch.
By the time they are through with what is left of you,
it is clear they have forgotten what it is you once were
when you were once in the quiet in the coral and fell
breathing in the morning air.

SMALL TREE AT CALIFORNIA GAS STATION

Oh to be this small tree planted in a pot in the shade
at a Shell gas station in Agoura Hills, California.
You're out in nature; you're just outside of Los Angeles;
nothing could ever be better. "How many celebrities
have you seen? How's the sunshine and surf?"
The roots back home, where you got plucked,
all want souvenir tees, sweatshirts, bags, mugs.
They'll have you to show them the Santa Monica Pier,
those limited cares and unlimited views.
Stilt walkers and fire jugglers. "Paradise," in other words.

You say no one really swims out that way.
Too much wastewater and sewage spills.
Grosser than its *Grand Theft Auto* counterpart.
Would you want to see the Hollywood Sign on fire instead?
And the protests, the strikes, unemployment, unaffordable,
all the unhoused people clinging to that pier for support—
these aren't landmarks, necessarily,
no keychain for the pain,
but we could check them out, if you'd like, and take pictures.
Let everyone online know you made it, because.

You are the tree planted at the gas station, frigid in the dark
on the Ventura Freeway, where the voyagers and vagabonds
ask the smarter question: "Where ya headin', friend?"
How on earth do you answer that?

WRITTEN UPON LEARNING CLEOPATRA DIED BY SUICIDE BY HAVING A COBRA BITE HER ON THE BOOB

Y'know what, Cleo? I get it. Who hasn't been there?
Life's hard. Sometimes your ex-boyfriend's adopted
son decides to kidnap you to humiliate you, and rather
than going through all that tragicomedy, hey, better to
just have a cobra bite you on the boob. The boob!
Bet Caesar wishes that were him. 'Cept he's dead too.
Assassinated. A titillating history, those Egyptians.
And oh to be that cobra! What a conversation starter!
I bit the boob of the last Hellenistic pharaoh—and you?
Imagine a wine night with Medusa, Quetzalcóatl,
the Garden of Eden serpent, Hercules's Hydra,
Kaa from *The Jungle Book*, and this charmer here.
There needs to be more positive snake representation.
Snakes want to shed their skin of these stereotypes—
sorry, s-s-s-sorry, had to. Here's your representation:
Cleopatra VII Thea Philopator refused to be a prisoner
to Octavian's rule, and her husband Mark Antony had
already died in her arms. So she sent for this cobra,
met eyes with the very creature no man can tame,
admired the power he held. Then pressed him to her.
Fangs against breast; his venom, her authorship.

He did his duty to his country, answered to his queen.
But yes, was probably hanged for it after. And when
Medusa, Quetzalcóatl, and the others all gather for
our cobra's burial, may they smile at his sarcophagus.
May they say, At least he went out doing what he loved.

MYTH OF MYSELF

Floating aimlessly in a pink donut inflatable
like a logo in a DVD pause screen
while the rest of the world goes to shit.
Where is something.
Not anywhere.
Spiraling, yes, but descending? Ascending?
Swimming in circles.
Can't live off my royalties much longer.
Do you remember I used to write books?
What happened to those characters?
Too many free shots at the house bar
and pool parties
and sun-reddened chests
and cocktail flus
and coasting up the soak.
My delusions used to empower me.
Now I'm just trying to make a living.
I am a phone plugged into its charger
that is not plugged in to the wall.
You are the shapeshifter. I am the hunter.
Nothing's free or forgiven.

WATCHING A NATURE DOCUMENTARY WHILE YOUR ROOMMATE HAS SEX DOWN THE HALL

Do you know about the pistol and stamen in flowers?
Or maybe it's *pistil* and stamen—
excuse me, got distracted there. Here's what I'm learning.
There's a rainforest in the verdant valleys of Asia
where one tree species grows taller than all the rest,
with spikes on its bark and poison that drips down it.
No predators would dare go near that tree.
So it thrives above the canopy, eating all the sunlight.
But the migratory birds like the wonderful and wild view too.
Great spot to mate. Tucked away, cackling loudly—
hold on, let me turn up the volume. Shoot me.
Not in the best of moods. In high school, I used to say
my favorite color was robin's-egg blue.
Now I don't give a shit. Green is fine.
Looking at green is good for your eyes.
But the birds, they shit all over that tree, don't they?
And all the bird droppings pile high beneath that tree,
which no predator settles by because of its poisonous spikes.
The droppings are toxic to the soil. Roots can't survive.
Nutrients don't make it all the way up to the top.
So the branches fall, one by one,

and then last, the tree. Into the green shadows.
What protects it destroys it, living with regret—
wait, sorry, forgot how vocal she can get.

MR. JOHN JAMES AUDUBON (1785–1851)
(After Fabien Grolleau)

*Hopes are shy birds flying at a great distance,
seldom reached by the best of guns.*

—JOHN JAMES AUDUBON, 1810

Alone in New Orleans, his wife and sons home in Kentucky,
Audubon—Fougère, Laforêt, Jean-Jacques, or John James—
starves among his paintings and his Carolina parrot carcasses
to afford pink pastels to finish the flamingos next.

Over one hundred birds per day he's killing to make his art:
to inspect their stomach linings; to study their plumage colors;
to pose them, propped on sticks with others of their kind,
so that he may capture their likeness in brilliant illustrations.
Audubon crossed Mississippi, Alabama, Florida for these birds.

Over one hundred birds per day he's killing to make his art:
to present his pictorial records to his academic colleagues;
to receive no support for his ecological exercises, on the basis
of coming in second to earlier ornithologist Alexander Wilson.
Audubon is ridiculed, discarded, told to paint portraits instead.

Oh to be Audubon—his involvement in slavery aside—
with his passion for the American wildlife so colossal and rare
that he would destroy what he loves to preserve it for others,
that he would shoot at least seven of those Carolina parrots
so that we may imagine how this extinct species once lived.

Naturally, this is how we as poets also portray our subjects,
how we kill our darlings. Flamingos of the most perfect pink.

A TEXTUAL TOUR OF MY *ANIMAL CROSSING* ISLAND BASED ON MEMORY

The island of Sea Breeze is haunted, wreathed in mist,
perpetually a postcard to coastal Christmases past.
Villagers include a squirrel, a frog, a koala, others.
There are stalls where I pretend these animals sell
homemade holiday baubles and baked goods to visitors.
Tourism supports our sleepy, cobblestoned economy.
We have a full museum, a general store, a tailor.
A cemetery too, with mossy statues and a grave for
Soleil: an orange gerbil lost at sea in 2020. They say
you'll find the contents of her purse washed up onto shore
some early winter mornings. Red lipstick. Mascara.

Beyond town awaits the evergreen-bristled woods.
A campsite. A hammock with a typewriter, mine.
And my charming cottage with its back room dedicated to
Soleil: lit candles everywhere, a white grand piano,
a scintillating chandelier, a somber vibe to glamour shrine.
Her photo on the table. Memories of her being.
Yet out the window, on the northernmost shore, lies
Soleil's algae-encrusted skeleton, home to the sandworms.
Blue-gray waves break on towering cliffs.

Rumors of murder! Gossip of my involvement.
Why would I kill off Soleil?

The truth is less salacious. Soleil asked to leave.
So a pop-idol duck replaced her, and I missed her,
Soleil—and I'd spent eleven real-life days carving
this island to my every desire—it's a prop skeleton, okay?
I was bored. And I'm still so bored, these years later.
At a certain hour in the velvet night,
you just have to keep yourself entertained.
And the villagers all have me to blame.

ON THIS, THE ONE-HUNDREDTH REJECTION LETTER FROM WALT DISNEY STUDIOS, WE RECONSIDER THE MAGIC OF LATE-STAGE CAPITALISM

Dear Applicant. Thank you once again for applying to be a [production assistant, administrative assistant, executive assistant, development assistant, creative assistant, assistant to the head of creativity, assistant to the department of redundancy department, secretary] or whatever it was this time around. We value your time, but clearly you do not value ours. We send these perfunctory emails, months after the fact, so that you know we at least had our AI screen your resume for a job for which we have already chosen a candidate (whose mother works here and to whom we owe a favor) but listed for legal purposes and our shareholders. It's funny: Walt himself once said, "All our dreams can come true, if we have the courage to pursue them"—and *gawrsh*, what a load of pixie dust that was. At Disney, we believe in the power of dreams, yes, but we also believe yours was more like tossing a flip-flop at Cinderella's castle and hoping for the best. So, to commemorate your one-hundredth application (did you think there was a prize if you reached this number?), let us leave no room for misinterpretation: You will never work for Walt Disney Studios. Who even told you employment here was possible? Our corporate website? Nice try. Not even

an interview. Buy a ticket to the theme park and eat yourself a churro instead. Why would you—what possessed you to even apply here? Your childhood? Michael Mouse? Please. Your top-five, desert-island, all-time favorite Disney movies are, in order: *Tarzan, Lilo & Stitch, An Extremely Goofy Movie, The Little Mermaid II: Return to the Sea*, and *Holes*. Are you for real. What the hell. We know exactly when you grew up; you don't even remember 9/11. We were there for 9/11. And if we weren't, well, hey, we work for Walt Disney Studios and you don't! Never will! You're ugly! Rot in hell! At least this time we're honest. We're working with magic, kid, not miracle hires. You want the same crap we sent you earlier? *If you are still interested in becoming part of the Disney story, check out DisneyCareers.com to keep applying for jobs that match your skills and talents.* Also, by the way, you will never bring children joy the way we once made you joyful, once upon a time. Robin Hood, Alice, Hercules, Quasimodo, Pocahontas. Yeah, we did that. Where were you? Where are you? Are you coming back? Will there be a one hundred and one? Of course you'd make the Dalmatian joke. Hey, how 'bout you take that crap to Warner Bros. before we buy them too, huh? And hey. Hey, hey, hey, hey. Hey. We're sorry. Really, we are. That wasn't nice, was it? We love you. We love you! We always have. And, you'll watch our live-action *Tarzan* next year, won't you? In theaters? Good. You're doing such a good job. Maybe one hundred and one will be the one for you, but hey, so sorry, not this time—oh, and now we've got to go send another email to someone just like you. Just like you! So many of you down there. Anyway. We wish you all the best in your career pursuits, wherever your happily-ever-after may take you.
Same time next week?

ROOMMATES, PART TWO

Kassandra isn't drinking with me, because she's six years sober.
I'm on the verge of eviction, but she doesn't know that—
I won't let her know that. How dehumanizing. So I am drinking.

We're in my Burbank apartment: small, cozy, with bougainvillea-
draped balconies and succulents lining the windowsill.
It's so discreet, you could easily miss it. And I will.
But I need a job, and here's Kassandra from college
working as a development assistant down the street.
Drove over after work. We're a long way from Tulsa.
She says she loves my decorations, all to be packed up or tossed.
I'm so desperate, freaking out inside, is her company hiring—
I went from thirty thousand to nine hundred dollars total
in the breath of a year. The Hollywood strikes. Unemployment.
And Kassandra from college is at my table recommending I watch
Past Lives because she saw the film last week on streaming
and liked it a lot, she says, and I'm sweating and should eat
something but haven't been eating well at all the last month.
Kassandra says you would like the film too, and I show her again
the photograph of you and me from my wallet. Such a cute couple,
she tells me, though it doesn't feel that way these days, nothing cute
about this or how my hands won't stop shaking and I spill the wine
and like the asshole I am remind Kassandra that I haven't seen her
since that one night our junior year when she rammed her car
into Jonah's apartment—remember that? We'd been drinking

something, I say, and she had been making fun of her roommate
Hayley for potentially being pregnant even though she wasn't—
and whatever happened to Hayley Reynolds, Kassandra?
Did she turn out fine, did she "get over it" like you said she would?
Hayley and her boyfriend broke up, did you know that,
and doesn't she have a kid now with someone else?
And Jonah is in Burbank shooting short films and commercials,
and Kassandra is in Burbank doing *development assistanting*
or whatever, yeah, and Kassandra, hey, Kassandra, hey,
do you and Jonah ever run into each other out here, hmm—
do you ever run into Jonah and his apartment with your car
like you did when he broke up with you our junior year?
You fighting for his phone? Spitting in his face? The police?
Glass shattering? Someone screaming? Dogs barking distantly?

Kassandra rises, says people change a lot in their twenties.
She takes her jacket and leaves, and next week, so do I.
But it's fine, really. It's all fine! We'll get over it. Oh God.

OOPS! POETRY PAYWALL

You're *so close* to the next stanza!

You bought the book. Don't stop at the surface.

The best lines are still ahead—but they live in <u>Premium</u>.

You are on the Muses Tier:

Access to a limited number of chapters or poems.

Just enough to spark curiosity.

Unlock a new poem every two days...

Or subscribe now to keep the poetry flowing.

More depth. More meaning.

Now the words are reading you.

Finish what you started. Accomplishit™ today.

[Turn Page to Process Payment →]

NICE TO SEE YOU AGAIN ON THIS DATING APP

A year later and you're twenty-four instead of twenty-three.
Moved out of Malibu, I see, but still from Hawaiʻi,
with the Mount Waiʻaleʻale waterfalls you told me about.
How you used to eat hamburgers layer by layer.
How you love sour candy and fear your ex-boyfriend.
The week you and I were messaging,
he took a pair of jeans you had bought him,
cut out the zipper, and then left it on the hood of your car.
Not sure the statement he was trying to make there.
You: Aquarius, vaccinated, plucky surfer girl,
the sand your catwalk, remote, reclusive.
Texts to me about the time you cut your clit in half
the first time you skateboarded, or when your dad
accidentally drove a rental car down a flight of stairs in Greece.
Or even when your aunt entered you into the logrolling
competition at the 2009 Escanaba State Fair. You won!
And—what happened to Santa Monica, really?
Weren't we meant to browse that new bookstore, the café?
I guess I didn't do my part to follow up either.
I was mixed with someone else. Then by myself.
Then many, many months spent working on myself.

Different photos, same smile. Your profile says,
"I recently discovered the world doesn't revolve around me."
I'm still learning. At the time, my buddy Nolan said that
a year from now, I won't even remember you.

HYDRATING THROUGH THE FIVE STAGES OF GRIEF

And waddling back to the cottage after my shift at the resort.
Sticky in my concierge blazer, half-dead on champagne
and orange juice, feeling the heat of an August afternoon.
Grapefruit, lemon, and apple trees. I fall back onto that
long couch in the hallway and pull a paperback over my eyes,
these pages that feel like old friends. A fly keeps me up.
Out of paper towels. Johnny comes by, reeking of his weed,
and he asks if he can watch *SpongeBob* on the TV.
Just walks in here like that to watch my scratched DVD
of *SpongeBob SquarePants* season two—sure, okay, bud.
So he sits on the second long couch while I rest on mine.
Names in the credits I recognize, all out of work.
We keep the door open so the fly can get home to its family.
In the fridge, the mojitos from yesterday's midnight UNO.
Johnny calls the girl he's seeing, shows me her picture after.
I met her once at a house party across the street,
when she tried to smoke weed out of my taquito.
He laughs like the yellow sponge. "Taq-*weed*-o."
The hell's wrong with me? Or that one Petco goth girl—
who made me believe wine tasted better under certain moons,
who made me believe I was her favorite punching bag.
She didn't want to be exclusive with me, she got married after,
and then she started up her own mobile pet grooming company.
And good for her. Won't make that mistake twice. 'Cept I do.

Call it life experience, alive in this living room of long couches
where I miss my German friends, meant for a semester singular
but stayed abroad for two. We went to Yosemite together
and would have late-night conversations on these couches
about public policy and fast fashion. They returned to reality
while I stayed in the dream, hiking, hot-tubbing, hallucinogens.
Kicked Evan off these couches—probably the kick he needed.
Hope he's doing better. I close my eyes and ignore all the shit
he pulled toward the end, and I swear I can see us driving home
after pizza, pulling off to the side of the road, and then blasting
Def Leppard and Pink Floyd as the sky turns citron yellow.
Which is something people say when their time has passed.
Wine Wednesdays in this living room. A bunch of other friends.
I don't have any new notifications. And it's not even evening,
and the cushion is cool beneath my head, and I swear to them
all I am falling asleep for real this time.

YOUR LIFE BETTER

A simple iMessage game of pool.
It's the game-finishing shot,
the eight ball in the top-left corner.
It's a delicate shot,
very delicate,
there—
and the ball rolls into the hole.
I won!
But wait?

When the move sent to my friend,
the eight ball didn't sink.
Rolled up to the edge instead.
The exact same move
went differently on our two screens.
One world.
Two realities.
Am I in the wrong one?
To this day I wonder.

If I like your life better,
then your life better be worth it.

II. SEARCHING

TIME TRAVEL

My eight-year-old self would wonder whether
I became a journalist or a jungle explorer.
He'd want to know how my cousins are doing
and maybe my sister, who was two at the time.
If I have a dog like Scooby-Doo.
No questions about my mother, probably,
because I assumed then my momma was fine;
I'd yet to watch her cry on the phone in the garage.
This would be just before my parents separated.
A perennially summer space.
He and I'd talk worms and dandelions
and why there would be seashells in the red dirt
all the way here in landlocked Oklahoma.
Was it proof God had once flooded the earth?
Will it happen again?
And toads, turtles, acorns, boats, willow trees.
I acted out adventures with my action figures,
watched PBS Kids, and played Neopets online.
I was curious and wanted to see new worlds—
or create them if I couldn't.
I was lonely.
So I imagine I'll be talking to myself for a while.
I'll want to know if I have a wife, what her name is.
What California is like. And what's after. ෴

SUMMER ELSEWHERE

Do you remember when we were kids and all gathered
at the pool that one summer, running around with ice pops?
Do you remember the lazy river and our conversation on it?
The giant waterslides. How tan we'd get playing pirates.
Didn't they take us there by bus ride—did that happen?
Together? I know my mom was working her new job,
my dad nowhere to be found and dangerous anyway.
But this place was safe. A church? What was its name?
And our friends, where did they go? Who were they?
All the computers had Windows XP, the boys all dirty feet.
Afternoons of a hamster anime and *Super Smash Bros. Brawl.*
I'm trying to remember, I'm sorry, I swear that I am.
It was important to me then; I don't want to let you down now.
The adults—please, was there a Jennifer? Amanda? Mr. Man?
I can't recall the context, but Mr. Man once let it slip
he drinks beer, and I do remember I shamed him so much for it,
and how was he supposed to defend himself, really,
to this eight-year-old Christian kid? What could he have said?
He'd laugh so hard if he knew what I drink now.
We all played duck, duck, goose and tag in the grass,
when I'd yet to be defined by a singular idea—
and I will never get that back except for right here,
in this reading. In this reading, I am eight years old,
and I will never drink beer, and for a whole summer
I can pretend to be a pirate. Somedays I still am.

MIDDLE SCHOOL ADVICE, 2008

The lockers are very tiny, so I suggest you make things fit as best you can. School food is nast exept for there pizza. Packing your own lunch is always better. There are some very strange and mean people, but if they say something try to ignore them. You have seven classes with only 5 minutes between each, so use that time at you locker or getting between classes. Teachers get mad and you will probably be late if you don't do this. Isn't it strange that my french teacher requires a mechanical pencil. No teachers like them. My orchestra teacher hardly ever shows up. When she's gone, we get to watch tv and movies. That is almost every day. One of the substitute teachers got fired because he cussed a kid out. Have you been watching american idol. Some strange people trying out. Emily is in orchestra with me. We both play the viola. I HATE ORCHESTRA WHEN THE TEACHER IS THERE. I am making all As and Bs in school. The classes are much larger. You will have WAY to much homework, which will consume most of your time when you get home.(not every day) It is a lot harder than elementary, so be prepared. There are a lot more people like you, so everybody allways makes more friends in middle school. The bathrooms are disgusting because people write things everywhere, they don't flush' it smells nasty, and many other reasons. Personaly, I like middle school better than elementary. It may sound realy bad after all of this, but there are some good things about it too. More friends, languages, and much more. Does that sum it up enough? I just saw a shark stomach on tv. Ewe ewe ewe. LOL :]

YOUTUBE OF OUR YEARS

In the video, from the point of view of a handheld camera,
a bunch of thirteen-year-olds are fretting at the base of a tree.
Up the old oak, a couple of boys are too high for comfort.

The female friends call up to them: "Don't die on us!"
An ugly pit bull scampers past, a ball in her mouth.
Then the videographer climbs too, into the branches and feet.
Someone asks, "What the crap are you guys doing?"
"They're climbing a tree—what do you think they're doing?"
"Okay, this is as high as I'm going!" "Don't fall!"
"I can't make any promises!" "Stop dropping things on me!"
"Can you come up here and tie my shoe?" "Tie them together!"
"This is an awkward position." "Call the fire department!"
"Are you taping this whole thing?" "My brother did that once."
"Jump from a tree?" "Yeah, for a girl he wanted to do."
"What is with you children and climbing things?"
"I gotta film this!" "You guys are my source of entertainment,"
and other overlapping shouts and exclamations.

It is a December weekend and we're in eighth grade.
The videographer reaches the top branch, with me on it.
My Converse is untied. Some things never change.

FACEBOOK MESSAGES, 2011

Full-on conversations, with hellos and goodbyes between them. Also sharing YouTube videos, and chatting about the upcoming *Harry Potter* movie, and listening to Radiohead and The Killers. He has a slider cell phone. She's converting CDs into audio files into MP3s. Over two thousand songs on her iPod. It's common for them to be on Facebook after school, messaging friends.

In February, she says she's deciding whether to take a regular art class or an advanced art class once they get to high school. The advanced art class would be more serious, she says, but she has no interest in going to an art college. He says she can decide on commitment later. She says she'll probably take the normal art class. She ends up getting her master's in fine arts.

In March, they're talking about geometry homework, and she says Hana needs to talk to Nick more. He says they're doomed. She says she hopes not. He asks her why Abraham deactivated his Facebook. She says she heard it's because Abraham wanted to work out more, but she doesn't know what working out has to do with Facebook. He asks if she's going to the school dance.

In April, she says hi and asks how he is. He suggests she talk to Alan instead. She says she doesn't need to spend all her time texting Alan, that she can still talk with other people. Also her phone is dead. She asks if he likes Rowan, a girl in their classes.

He evades the question like his life depends on it, and maybe it did back then. She tells him it's perfectly normal to like somebody.

In May, she gets her braces off, and he and Rowan are dating. She says he's lucky she hasn't teased him like he's teased her. Then they're arguing—she's acting b*****, he's being an a******. He says he doesn't even know who she is anymore. She says she's been wondering the same. She says she'd rather him talk to her and make her feel bad than him not talk to her at all. He says he'll call.

In June, they are arguing again. He asks how Rowan is doing. She says she doesn't know and to give Rowan space. They talk God. Then she tells him he overreacts and takes relationships too seriously for their age, that he blames people, that he inserts himself into people's lives and doesn't seem to care about their feelings as much as his own. That he hides behind technology.

She asks him to never call her a b**** again. He says he forgot he did that, then he apologizes for it. He says he doesn't want to remember this fifteen years from now. She says it's okay. And that he should wait to talk to Rowan again until school starts. And that she's going to hockey camp tomorrow. And she'll be back in time for his birthday. He says he's looking forward to it.

In late August, at high school's beginning, he gets a message from a different user, the account long since deactivated. This user claims to have known of a girl who'd had a crush on him in middle school. He guesses one girl. In the chat, the user says they swore they'd never say. He asks again. The user reveals nothing. The user says: I guess you'll never know.

RUBIES

I was fifteen, she was sixteen.
I'd heard about a party over the weekend
where she cried as her equally drunk
friends tried to get her to eat,
and then the next morning,
she vomited with such force
in her friend's shower
that said friend had to explain
to her grandma that the girl
just had bad asthma and no,
really, everything was fine.
She had a boyfriend, and I'd heard
he'd had sex with her other friend
in a hotel room
for his four buddies to watch and join in.

I'd found the self-deleting picture-sending app
everyone was talking about.
Downloaded, added strangers,
usernames from forums on the internet,
and I sent myself to them.
They sent new cleavage, panties, tongues.
I tried using body wash soap as lubricant
before I knew what lubricant was.
Gave myself a red rash

that made my testicles look like rubies
before flaking off the following days
in front of a urinal.
The time did come,
and when I did, it was recorded by my phone
in my right hand.
That video's still unopened somewhere.

CATFISHING

It's been quite a while since I read your email. I honestly have no idea what to say anymore. Not that I really had an idea any other time I've emailed you. It feels like a "my whole life is a lie" moment more than anything. Obviously, my whole life isn't a lie, but the part involving my knowledge about you, well, it's a bit hard to wrap my head around. I suppose that's the beauty of the internet, then. You can genuinely recreate yourself. I find it insane how quickly I put you on a pedestal. I was under the impression that you were older, mature, more experienced, someone who could advise and guide me. That impression is just gone now, along with the pedestal you stood on for, what, four years? I feel rather naïve, foolish really, and I simply cannot forgive you for making me feel like that. I always expected something, some lie I would see through; I always questioned every piece of information you'd given me, but still I just so wanted to believe in the image I'd formed around those pieces. Maybe it was all in my head. Maybe I was just being silly. But four years! I've always told myself I know absolutely nothing about you, nothing for sure, and now it feels like even less than that. I know now that the person underneath it all is just that, one person. I'll admit that though I was hurt learning we're the same age, I was also oddly excited. Maybe it's because it seems like I would more easily relate to you; I'm really not sure. But perhaps I just need to adjust to the fifteen-going-on-sixteen, slightly nerdier image of you. This changes things. And I'm sure you're aware of that, but for me, personally, it changes a lot. Are you even from Oklahoma? I guess that doesn't matter. Whether you're Bryant or Sebastian or Griffinity (though I'm guessing Bryant is the real one as I look over your Facebook), it's been a decent four years knowing you. And I'm honestly so happy I had someone to at least have our conversations with during those four years. I know about half the time you were joking, but when you were serious, it meant the most to me. At one point, I hoped that in some weird way we would meet each other in real life and not know it. Strange, I know. I still wish it could happen.

ABE

I just saw someone. I was walking the dog in the rain,
and in the dark under the neighborhood lamppost
was Abraham. He had his elephant lunchbox with him.
He looked the exact same since middle school—
I mean, *the exact same* since middle school.
That dark, curly hair of his, and his long legs,
and the exaggerated walk he'd do to make us laugh
on the track. Those humid afternoons.
When did I last see Abe? Before or after his dad died?
I don't remember how I'd heard that had happened.
I don't remember telling him so sorry. I must not have.
That must have been, what, ten years ago, maybe?
And I don't remember his birthday, just that
he never wanted anyone to know when it was.
Uncomfortable with the idea of any obligation, he said.
I spent the night at Abe's after the eighth-grade dance.
We talked about the same girl. His dad made us oatmeal.
Abraham and I both were clever, but I was unkind.
And I hated Abraham, later, in our high school years.
The weird, funny guy, bouncing from girl to girl in our
friend group, no matter who they were already dating.
Texting them winking faces and innocent innuendos.
He did dumb stuff and got dumb laughs because of it.
That Halloween party when the girls straightened his hair
and did his makeup, brushing arms, spin the bottle

and shrooms at the lake and the girls in the bedroom
and whatever happened at that pool party senior year—
it's like he didn't know what he wanted at all
and so was trying anything he possibly could.
It's like he, well, maybe, and what I saw, who he was—
he had an older brother around the house, maybe,
who'd had a shitty first relationship, or drugs, or,
or maybe I felt this way because we were both sharing
the same spotlight, both craving positive responses,
bouncing around those girls like we didn't know better,
and we did. Of course we did. There we were, he and me,
two people self-defined by the reactions of others,
two lonely, too quiet, too loud, too teenage. Boys.
Abraham was there. Then he wasn't. Just shadows.
Looks like it's stopped raining. And there's the moon.

"THE DEAD" BY JAMES JOYCE

He longed to be master of her strange mood.

Gabriel, preoccupied with his public image,
feels pressure to give a toast at a Christmas party
in Dublin. Yet he delivers a flawless speech
at this dinner, surrounded by loved ones
who admire his wit, good looks, and charm—
but he is embarrassed by his wife Gretta's
emotional reaction to a piano piece from upstairs.
She recomposes herself and apologies to him.

A blizzard forces the couple to stay in Dublin.
Gabriel criticizes Gretta as they prepare to sleep.
Gretta apologizes again and explains, weeping,
that a man she was once engaged to had died
in a similar snowstorm while bringing her soup,
and he used to play for her that same piano piece.
Gabriel realizes then his wife and everyone else
have full lives, beyond him, haunting him.

At least, that's how I recount the narrative.
It's a story I came across a decade ago—
three days after my girlfriend in high school
ended our relationship. I haven't read it since. ❧

THE FAULT IN OUR EXPECTATIONS

I was seventeen, and everything felt like it mattered
more. Remember? We typed "lol" without laughing.
The Wi-Fi was trash, but we passed notes through
Tumblr reblogs and Snapchat anyway. Our dreams
filtered, our heartbreaks hidden behind hashtags.
We still used Facebook, barely. Teachers called us
distracted, but we were just scared this math test was it.
My iPhone 6. Indie bands and college applications.
The occasional "you good?" from Jared in the middle
of AP Psych. No one notices you disappearing except
maybe the attendance sheet. Slowly, like buffering.
We shared sad quotes in typewriter fonts, believed
we were broken in beautiful ways. Who to sit with.
What to say. How to eat without anyone observing—
or worse, not at all. September afternoons on the roof
of the high school with Alan, Ally, Rowan, Hana, Nick.
We read *To the Lighthouse*, and I underlined a sentence
about trees and changing leaves that I didn't understand
but felt was important. What was I doing with my hair?
My friend Abraham said he was going to "start over"
in college, as if one could uninstall the version of us
that cried at three a.m. over a message that never came
or did. *Move to California. Get out. Be better. Anything.*
I think I wrote "forever" in a lot of yearbooks to friends
I don't speak with, about feelings too big for a body

that still couldn't drive without asking permission first.
I spent too many December nights staring at the ceiling
of my bedroom, trying to figure out if I was the problem
or just really bad at texting, googling how to stop being
a background character in my own adolescence, yes.
My best friend Mary Faith. I had hoped someday we'd
fall in love by accident, because that's what happens in
books written by adults trying to remember being a kid,
like now. No one stood on a table; no one declared love;
no voice-over explained me. No manic pixie dream girl
to teach me how to live my life before she vanished into
metaphor and mid-April humidity. I sure didn't drive
a hearse or read Whitman for fun or play pranks on the
entire school as some sort of social commentary, no.
I existed. Half in love with the idea of mattering, half
terrified someone might notice me for who I really am,
like my actual girlfriend, with flirty texts and parties
and how enchanting she looked on our prom night.
But all I got was a B-minus in chemistry. I don't know.
Our lives were built on countdowns: a hundred days till
graduation, fifty days till college decisions, two weeks
until I never see these people again, and I never do.
Then the parking lot, June sun too bright, watching a girl
cry while pretending not to. I'm still not sure what any
of it meant. Just a kid, with shaky hands, writing a novel
in the back of math class while waiting for a future
I couldn't quite imagine but believed in.

TO SLEEP IN SPITE OF SEA; OR, THE GHOST OF WINDHAVEN BEACH

Well, I heard she walks the shoreline just before the sky turns.
I heard her head hit the rocks so hard the sea turned black.
I heard her scream never stopped, just sank.
I heard she comes back when the moon is paper thin, the wind wrong.
I heard you'll smell salt and rust before you see her.
I heard she leaves claw marks in the driftwood.
I heard phones will lose signal when she's breathing behind you.
I heard she was a student at the high school and everyone knew her.
I heard the ocean kept her heartbeat and plays it during thunderstorms.
I heard she hates couples who hold hands too tight.
I heard hermits live there because she lets them bury knives to calm her.
I heard the water won't touch her, only follows.
I heard she was only sixteen when the ocean wrote her down.
I heard she's waiting for a different ending.
I heard she has no interest in being seen or heard.
I heard she haunts a hotel—no, that's a movie from the eighties.
I heard she made a storm reverse direction just to ruin a wedding.
I heard she touches nothing but leaves sea glass in a row.
I heard her voice can be heard in the hush between the waves.

I heard if you whisper a secret on that beach, she'll listen, she'll keep it.
I heard a man comes each summer, always alone, sighing his apologies.
I heard she drips seaweed onto pillows at night.
I heard she presses her face to windows, eyes wide, mouth full of water.
I heard you can't move when she looks at you, not even if you try.
I heard her name was Saphnie.

THEY WILL KNOW THE TRUTH

She yelled at me when he came to himself;
they did it because we said no.

She yelled when he came back;
they did not enter because of unbelief.

She yelled, "More, more, more!"
when he came back, and there was no light
because they did not receive the love of the truth.

And she yelled, "God!"
when he came up out of the water
because they did not love the truth.

And the truth did set us free.

HEART'S MEMORY

I'm forgetting a lot, I'm finding. That I'm forgetting.
Worries and wants that had seemed so large when I was
younger, but I don't, can't, remember the specifics
——————, unless I happened to write it down.
What I wrote becomes what happened. Blends.
I know a September 2nd, but whose birthday was that?
I know making out with a girl sophomore year
and the excitement in seeing her white-lace bra,
but did that happen to me, or to one of my protagonists?
How could I ever forget what Bryna looked like?
An entire poetry book and I never once described her eyes.
It was the drinking or the trauma response or the years—
I'm losing *something* and I can't tell what that was.
It hurts.
Maybe it all was meant to be forgotten. I'm next in line.
And so if it is true what I write becomes what happened,
then what happened was anything you'd like.
Peter Pan and dear Wendy. Manta rays like giant kites.
What happened was the twenty of us gathered around
that bonfire at the beach with our hot dogs and s'mores,
that brief September interlude when the sun goes down
and the temps are cool enough to put on a sweatshirt,
and we share ghost stories and we poke fun and we eat—

and maybe in the tent later that night, I see a white-lace bra
and her eyes, which are warm like the sun shining
on a riverbed in the late-summer woods. I stumble
the wrong words, I'm sure, and this time it won't matter.

MARRYING MY GIRLFRIEND FROM HIGH SCHOOL

A week before my twenty-first birthday,
I dream it's our wedding day.
Carlos is there, Ethan Bradford, Myles Murdock,
and even Maureen and her boyfriend—
but you don't know her, do you?
Our friends from high school are not
in attendance; I imagine they don't approve.

I imagine this is the type of dream only adults can have.

You and I are undeniably in love—
me, walking down the aisle in a suit
a bit too big, and you, at my side
in an off-white sleeveless dress,
the kind you might wear on a picnic date
or for brunch in town. Look at these two kids,
so sure of everything.
Your father doesn't walk with you—
he's not there, and I don't ask about it.
We stroll hand in hand instead, as equals.

The church sanctuary is more like a courtroom,
with your mother on one side
and mine on the other. My mom once admitted

to me she didn't like you, believed it was
you who broke my heart and not the other way
around. Here, though, she's supportive,
clapping politely at all the right moments.
She doesn't cry.

In this universe, we don't bring up
the past few years and what we went through
separately in college. We laugh and joke
and playfully shove each other.
After the ceremony, you wear my jacket
for the pictures. I kiss your neck, your lips.

And I suppose, then, I won't go to grad school
in California. You and I will move into
a little apartment in Tulsa—or maybe
the Pacific Northwest to finish your degree.
I get a job at yet another bookstore.
We come home at night, eat home-cooked pasta,
binge-watch your British reality TV together.
Same as before, but this time, we are good.

Instead, I awake in the blue-veined dawn,
your kind of blue, in the warm sunshine
of a perfect summer day.
Heartbeat quickens. The wedding, I don't want it
to have been real. But sometimes—
I sit there, the line between
chaos and security blurred, these
twinkling reflections in the corner of my eye
and the slumbering seeds of a dream.

THE WEILANDERS
(from *EverbladeOnline.com*)

Seb and I've set up camp behind someone's ransacked villa on a tawny, velvet beach. A small fire, blue-toned cushions, barefoot nonchalance, and what we pretend is dark rum. We're where heaven meets earth, the best of land and sea, with a sylvan backdrop and this warm water before us. The evening light, dappled by storm clouds, silhouettes the mountain peak and glows like butterscotch.

"How about: Arizona or Nevada?" Seb asks.

"Easy," I say. "Nevada. Give me those aliens."

A flash of green shoots across the sky—a somnambulist god rocking the coast—then vanishes as quickly as it appeared.

We discuss for several minutes the spacecrafts I believe I saw as a kid. Huge, dark, blending in with the night sky but given away by many lights flickering on the bottom. Triangular. Silent and hovering. I locked my window and couldn't sleep. All my memories of abduction are blurry red, but they don't feel like dreams. Some are painful and hard to describe, but they're mostly just me in strange white rooms with faceless beings and made to fill out papers with a name that isn't my own. "At least," I tell Seb, "I think they weren't people."

"And you're scared of them?" Seb asks. "The dots in the sky?"

"The controllers of the dots. But I'm ready either way."

Sebastian is a six-foot toddler trying his best. Outdated glasses, really nice eyebrows, clothes stolen from an anime phase. A golden trash bag. Twenty-seventh president William Howard Taft as a young man, kindhearted to the point of being gullible. Honestly, he's prettier than me.

"Agree to disagree," he says, grinning.

"And what do I look like?"

He puts a hand to his chin and nods his head, thinking it through. It's been nearly ten years since we last saw each other—before high school, before social services. Seb was an anarchist, but he helped me through it, late into those nights, with whispered assurances and soothing hushes, and I would always appreciate him for that. I am past dissociating while listening to music, above writing self-insert fan fiction, compulsive lying, my shoplifting days, doing exactly what people told me not to do behind their backs. But still I put active energy into avoiding all my problems until they come crashing down on me. I have nothing to show for anything, surrounded by invisible walls. And just as I've forgotten the question, Seb says: "You're a cranky witch exiled to the swampiest swamp."

"Not bad, but I have no chin. Witches have those chins."

"Some kind of witch-type villain, then." He laughs. "You live alone in a lair in the woods with your familiars and your garden of creepy vines. Not necessarily evil, just eccentric and misunderstood and with a track record of questionable decisions."

"Maybe I had a rough past."

"Maybe you want an excuse to practice your cackle."

Instead, I'm a beige cryptid with shoulder-length red hair, frequently seen wearing a black top hat. My favorite shoes are white cowgirl boots with fringe. Pirate smile. The girl of your dreams? I genuinely don't know. Not in the utmost health. I'd imagine myself to be this tanned, rainforest-type ethereal woman with blue eyes, green markings, and a friendly aura around her.

Wouldn't that be nice.

A momentary lull in the conversation. The water gently laps and tumbles over jungle-swathed rocks, purls back into the sea, and then the sun, too, ripples over it. The sound through my headphones is crisp. Vibrant.

Seb looks at me with half-lidded lust. I attempt to skip a stone, but it only rises into the sky. We scrape against the electrical matrix—a confusing metaphor with no elaboration.

But then we're back to discussing everything except that which matters most because I am too afraid to say goodbye. Atoms, aliens, magic, intellect, faraway galaxies, memories on this low-poly beach, the lies we told, Alabama versus Wyoming. Alabama seems awful, based purely on assumption. I would never voluntarily travel there; Alabama's flag must have a big red X for a reason. Whenever I see someone with Alabama plates, it's like, ugh, here we go.

"This world ain't big enough for both me and Wyoming."

"*Wyoming*. Why is it spelled like a verb? How does one wyome?"

Even as I wait here with Seb, half-asleep by the warmth of the embers, I know he is long gone. Yet this is my shoreline, my Sebastian, my sanctuary, my second life.

I must find *anything* to keep the fire from slowing to a single flame.

"What do you miss most?" I ask him.

"Mushrooms," he tells me, "growing on a log."

"Hey, I'm serious."

"I use a wheelchair," Seb says. He draws a circle in the sand with his feet. "Haven't been outside in months."

"Oh," I say. "I'm sorry. Did I know that? I don't remember if I knew that."

"Talking on the phone with a friend," he continues, "and losing track of time. When a cat or a dog has been sitting in a sunny spot for a while, and then you go to pet them, and you can feel the heat off their fur. Or when you were a kid watching for school closings because of a snowstorm and yours finally scrolled onto the screen."

"When you're driving on a road with a lot of traffic lights and make it through every single one without stopping."

"Stuff like that."

"Did you tell me, before, about you using a wheelchair?"

"No," he says. "Never came up."

Seb stands, alert, a hand on one of his throwing knives, and I follow his stare past the looming palms and Varisvaera coastline in the distance. We must look like ancient rock formations, huddled in the shrubbery, soaked in the rosy glow of the fire. Do we ever fully recover from the people we were at fourteen?

We're older, certainly, faces longer and with more wrinkles and acne scarring. I don't want to think how long it's been, even though that's all I do. Gone from memory are the faces to names like Kallistrate and Mountaines, or meanings of terms such as the kingdom of Weiland, the Tanesthesian empire, Folivora. I know I led the Battle of Yarborough, but who soldiered beside me? Who won the war? For the slaughtering of the White Wolves of Wisteria, I remember, they called me the Wolfslayer of Everblade. What is *Everblade Online* anymore?

Seb relaxes, and so we wallow at our oceanfront campsite. The sybaritic minimum. The dune grass sways in the breeze, and our names briefly flicker above our heads like fireflies.

I ask him how often he daydreams about being someone else. Because I do. Every day.

"Is that why we're still here?" he asks in return.

"Maybe. Being in just one body at one time feels so restrictive."

"It was fun," he affirms with such submerged attraction it must be true.

"This place started off as a safe space from real-life traumas. I could come and play for hours, be happy. Now I return to maintain that fantasy: all our achievements, the discord, the people we met, the worlds we discovered."

"I don't know," Seb says. "I was so combative and rude that I guess I'm glad I went through that as a kid because I know a lot of people now who get that way when they're adults and then never grow out of it. Probably kept me from going full-on hermit. This place made me feel important in a universe that didn't seem like it cared for me, and I can't thank it enough."

"Was it actually so much better back in the day? What do you remember?"

"That you were a nightmare. That I had a massive crush on you."

The feels, oh, the feels.

Sebastian was a username, a guardian type, had talked about meeting up at a motel once, on the border. Was he opinionated, sometimes annoyingly so? I have no idea. This place tricks my brain into thinking I'm socializing. I started playing when I was nine, and I'm twenty-two now. I just keep losing stuff and people, running in circles, and this world has been the only consistent thing I've had when everything else seems so uncertain.

I am a child.

I am in my bedroom, alone, playing a computer game, fighting alongside Seb, hyperventilating while an adult man and woman yell at each other on the other side of the wall. I try to ignore it, attacking, resisting, spinning my cutlass in the air with a flood of anger and dramatic flourish. A door slamming, my mother sobbing. The door to my room flings open, pouring in artificial light, as my father rushes up and turns me around to face him. He too is crying, says he loves me, that he will always love me, will always be my father, and that he is so, so sorry, Dera. He walks out on me still, and the screen is red.

"I wish I could go back," Seb tells me, "and treat the people I met here with more compassion and understanding. We were all struggling."

"Except now we're within this digital relic, multiple features defunct, stuck in the juxtaposition between the innocence of a kids' game and the experiences of its adult userbase. Our lives connect and disconnect—just like that."

"We lose each other, and we find ourselves again."

"We're here, and we're not."

"Now we're less than phantoms. Just some sort of forgotten data in the mass cyberspace."

"Illusion, elusion," and it probably doesn't matter who's speaking at this point.

Thunder crashes in the dark. Another flash. Abduction. Sebastian and I are stripped to our geometric shapes, then a slosh of pixels, a million fragments as the servers disconnect for the final time. We dissolve into a sprinkling of blue and green, stretching across this dream of ours, veering, twirling, and softening into the most gorgeous light.

"Today is my birthday," I whisper.

Seb laughs. "How horrible to spend it here."

We are death, debt, and depression in a twitchy, negative-image flashback—and yet, as he clasps what remains of a hand on my shoulder, I feel my lips play with a smile. This is the end screen: my own reflection. It's midnight at my apartment, and the electronics whir quietly, almost soothingly so.

I don't know if we won, but it is, at least, finished.

TWO BIRDS

Suzy and Sam walk past each other each day
on their way to work.
She smiles at him, and he waves to her,
but that is the extent of their exchange.

Suzy sits at home on Friday nights
with her cat and a good book.
Sam cooks himself a meal and watches shows
from his childhood.

Suzy and Sam walk past each other each day
on their way to work.
She waves to him, and he smiles at her.
What would you have them do?

NIGHT WINDOWS

Night windows pull me back to that bus ride in Ireland.
I was off to Cork, leaving her for just the weekend.
Then, "her" would be "you," but it's been too long.
Neither is there. Only my head against cool glass,
her playlist in my ears, a torn notebook page
in my jacket pocket telling me to *Come back safe*.
Outside the day dies and these hearts refuse.
So I thought. Soothing stops along the way.
It would be easy, too easy, to believe a young woman
in Dublin is waiting. That notebook was full of pages
sent to another I didn't know.

LAND OF FIRE AND ICE

Reykjavík lodge in winter, a hostel for
you, me, these Australians, too loud.
Have I seen them before?
Shouting about my thesis.
They're shouting about my thesis,
ecofeminist descriptions in Icelandic writing,
the last thing I want to talk about.
You're sleeping over.
You know I'm getting over
a cold and a Swede from last semester.
You're hiding from your own drama
you won't talk about;
you won't talk about a lot, with me.
We don't talk relationships.
We don't talk rationality or love.
We don't talk anything at all.
So I don't remember much as a person with you.
The punk-rock exhibit. Teaching me Björk.
Your shoulders, upper thighs,
our noses grazed, our position,
other reasons, elevating,
left and right, fire and ice, breast and brain,
beautiful and bleak, tight grasp of me—
you could've been anyone, really—

I couldn't hold it back any longer.
This is the modern world, I know,
and you're off to Monteriano next.
And I should be heading home.

VENTED VIEWS

Vented
views of
a coastal house
and the boyfriend
and girlfriend within.
Perhaps it's *girlfriend* and
boyfriend (excuse me); sure
seems that way, anyway. Look
for once. Stairs outside, leading
to the top deck, where she sunbathes,
her hand reaching up to shield her eyes
from (the glaring sun) her boyfriend, walking
up the inside stairs, holding on to the banister,
so orderly, so planar (so plain). Cool inside, air-
conditioned. He's fully clothed; she's not, but say,
is that a problem, hmm, if Mr. Neighborman sees?
No, she's in a striped one-piece, on a striped lawn chair, on
matching striped shadows from the outside stairs, the inside
stairs, the shadows from the banister, so parallel (so harsh, so
restrictive), when she's too (chaotic, disjointed, arched), and
the colors are so (cool), and the colors are too (cool), not (cool)
enough, sir, miss, anything...

And he's gone. Down the stairs. Where they don't care.
My God, do your stupid egos make one hell of a canvas.

HOW MANY TIMES HAVE YOU BEEN IN LOVE?

I think about my three-month relationship more
than I do my three-year relationship.
Fallen hard twice; everyone else was infatuation.
In college, there was an electrical engineer,
and she was fun, but she never introduced me
as hers, not even as a friend, just roundabout ways
that barely tied to her, and that bothered me.
It was so one-sided, and I was just love-ing,
on a different frequency or something.

Have you seen the movie *Eternal Sunshine
of the Spotless Mind*? There's a scene where
Jim Carrey's character is sitting in a diner,
and he sees Kate Winslet's character look at him
and then raise a coffee cup in a sarcastic gesture,
and he wonders to himself,
"Why do I fall in love with every woman I see
who shows me the least bit of affection?"
When the lack of attention is the driving force.

As a teen, I thought a bad headache was a migraine.
I thought I'd had a few. Then I did have a migraine.
I never knew what people meant by
"You'll know it when you feel it,"

but that's how I feel at this point. You'll know.
Oh—how many times have I been in *Iowa*?
Never, actually. Hadn't even considered it.
I hear downtown Des Moines becomes
a farmer's market on Saturdays in the summer.
Just live, laugh, love, Iowa.

RENT-A-FRIEND

The worst job I had was when I was a Rent-a-Friend.
Not for what it was but how it ended. For $25/hour,
people would rent me to be their friend or date for
social engagements—usually lonely guys and girls.
A woman's plus-one to her college friend's wedding.
A man's vent session over his work, his kids, his wife.

And then there was Lochlan, my age and awkward.
He needed a friend, and I was to be that friend.
His Malibu mother wanted to pay me $100/hour.
He had no idea. You know how this story ends.
Lochlan and I would play pool, rent bicycles,
explore Santa Monica and Venice Beach together.
Once, his parents paid me to spend the night with him
at their mansion while they took a romantic getaway.
Lochlan just wanted to order in food and watch movies.
Bullied in school, he'd turned to blockbusters to escape.
His favorite was *Frozen 2*. So for his birthday,
I bought him a plastic statue of that rearing, translucent,
mythical horse–water spirit from the movie.
Lochlan loved it. And then Lochlan wanted to hang out
every weekend. Then twice a week. Three times.
His calls were constant. He couldn't understand
I was a graduate student with class scripts to write,
actual dates to go on, my own friends to party with.

His calls were constant. I tried to set boundaries, but
this deal wasn't good, wasn't honest, wasn't worth it.
I deleted my Rent-a-Friend account and told his mother
she didn't have to pay me but needed to know I could not
see Lochlan as often as he wanted. Once a month, maybe.
I said I was lying to her son. She said I was performing.
His mother begged me to give Lochlan another chance—
that even though he can be overbearing, he means well,
she said, and he has no one. His calls were constant.
I told his mother she needed to tell Lochlan the truth
or I would. She offered money. Then the calls stopped.

After the Palisades Fire, I checked online and saw
Lochlan still had me blocked. But his mother hadn't.
The raging flames had destroyed their Malibu home
and everything inside. She posted a family picture from
their rental. In the background: the water spirit statue.
It wouldn't have survived fire. Lochlan took it with him.

RENT-A-FRIEND (POSTSCRIPT)

What really happened is less attractive.
What really happened is that
I texted Lochlan—Noah—
I needed a vacation from his
constant need for companionship.
I'd postcard him after, "maybe in a month,"
a promise tacked to the end like a postscript.
I didn't.
I was exhausted. There were only so many times
I could swim laps in that infinity pool;
I couldn't tell him the truth;
I couldn't watch *Frozen 2* forever.

It's Sunday how can you be busy
you have no classes on a Sunday

I never reached out again.
Nothing would survive that fire.

THINGS WE DON'T TALK ABOUT

The semesters I did coke in college
after my big breakup.
Vomiting in the shower, intoxicated,
sitting in it and just miserable.
How even though I meant to
keep things casual
with the flirty chemistry student
from the Ferris wheel that October,
I did develop feelings for her—
but I ignored them, for her, for me.
She and I had promised each other
we wouldn't be anything serious.
But then she did want to be serious.

I called it off entirely.
Call it self-preservation.
I thought I would move on. Couldn't.
She was sweet and heartbroken
and mailed me a letter
when I was so sick and alone.
She invited me to her graduation
the year after,
and that dress was familiar,
and we spoke for a minute,

and what we said stays between us,
and that was the end for us.

There are things I don't talk about
that were much more painful:
that wine night with Ashley,
those tequila nights with Leilani,
the lies I told and kept to let me
feel okay when I knew I wasn't.
At least those I'll name.
But the Ferris wheel girl—
she didn't do anything wrong.
She only wanted to see
if there could be more, for us.
I was too afraid.
What is there to say?

INTERMISSION

Deep breath. Nice. You've read, what, fortyish poems now?
Unless you just skimmed for the short ones—
no judgment. Actually, some judgment.
This here is not a poem. This is a pause dressed up as art,
the breathing room between poems that hit close to home
and poems that miss but ask for [APPLAUSE] anyway.
Let's admit it: this poetry? Was never going to heal you.
It was never designed to.
It's a mirror with *just enough fracture* to feel profound,
because self-awareness is cheaper than therapy
and sells better than sincerity.
Because the next poems are about love.
Or sex, or alcohol. Maybe all three.
Y'know, the hits.
Read 'em, don't read 'em; either way, you're holding a book,
and that's more than I can say for most of us.
And if you're still here: thank you. This book won't fix you,
but it just might keep you company. Could be that's enough.

WINE WEDNESDAYS

The wine nights start with a corkscrew and someone saying,
"Merlot again?" and a different friend laughing like the red
already hit. It's always the same hallway—long and narrow,
built to keep close. A kitchenette that knows our secrets,
a living room area with two long couches and extra chairs,
and a playlist spilling lo-fi jazz between conversations.
We call them Wine Wednesdays. We gather like ritual.
No one texts *Are you coming?* because of course we are.
Where else would we be? Here, in sophomoric metaphors,
punctuated by sips and accidental wisdom, a soft answer
to the loud loneliness that creeps between weekends.
Voices stacked on each other: *Are you still seeing him?*
Did you get the job? Hey, what if we ran away and bought
a ranch? This is Anastasia—she's into crystals and tarot.
Lucian studies butterfly geography—can you believe that?
Someone brings a bottle with a label they can't pronounce.
Someone's falling in love with a barista, or is mid-breakup.
The brave, the scared, the newly dumped, the freshly hired,
the maybe-I'll-move-to-New-York-someday dreamers.
We pass the bottle as communion, each swallow a surrender.
We toast to things we can't name: new starts, old flames,
the ache of almost-joy. As for me? I'm refilling glasses,
trying to read the night like a story with characters I adore.
It's the play of a Wednesday that pretends it's a Saturday.
And then, when our cheeks are flushed with the honesty hour

only red wine and dim light allow—we tumble to the hot tub.
Someone forgets a towel, someone wants to quit a job,
someone is laughing so hard they splash rosé into the water
and no one cares. Here, in the Burgundy bubble-hiss of dark,
we linger merry, unfinished, immortal, as the future waits
with real jobs and real cities and people we haven't met.
We know this is a gold-purple thing we don't get to keep.
Tonight, we hold the stars in trembling, tipsy hands and
dare them to burn as bright as we do: too young to know
how rare this is, just old enough to suspect it. We hold tight.
We pour one more glass. We climb into warmth like it can
preserve us, notes promising we'll do it again next week,
knowing full well the world won't always wait for us.
For us, we have wine. We have Wednesdays. We have
each other. For a moment, we have forever.

MARIE & MICHAEL

(from *Draw Me in to You*)

Loving a person is like art; it's in the details.

I love Marie. She colors me.
She's one of those lying-in-the-backyard
"tell me about your dreams" type of sunsets.
I love her cursive, her creativity.
She's the kind of calming
that comes wrapped in films or from
flipping through the pages of old books.
She'll smear chocolate on her teeth,
and I'll laugh with her nonsense.
Her drawings are not of people
as they see themselves
but what she loves most about them.
I used to starve myself of vulnerability—
I thought if I hurt myself
before the world got the chance, I'd be okay.
So I locked the good parts of me up,
and they've only been coming through my art
in bits ever since.
With her, I'm home, literally and figuratively.
Doing things to create love,
doing things through created love.

FEEDING TORTILLA CHIPS TO LITTLE BIRDS

This is your second-to-last chance, okay?
I said it's your third-to-last chance;
the freckles over your body won't draw
me in after that, won't want to imagine
constellations, dark mirrors, any longer.
Any longer, I would have been the father
to your children. How messed up they'd be.
How I can't be a father at this day and pay.
I'm trying to communicate my needs to
the universe. You don't even like me.
When was the last book you finished?
Why can't I buy any Sylvia Plath at the
supermarket but I can find ten—ten!—
copies of Hillary Clinton's memoir?
I voted for Hillary Clinton and would
rather reread *The Bell Jar*. Or the Bible.
Do you know Romans 12:18? *As much
as you can, so long as it depends on you,
live at peace with everyone.* How simple.
I cite that verse whenever someone asks
if I'm a Christian. Writers are less gods
than they are staff. Not believing their eyes,
they'd burn the sky; burn the entire sky!
Burn nothing. Only each other to keep us

warm—that stomach feeling of hope that the person in the room with you wants you there the same. You'll blame the astrology, I'm sure. And I've always been a Cancer.

NIGHT IN

She stumbles in, drops her bag,
laughs at nothing.
I watch from the kitchen.
Two glasses in the sink, both mine.
She asks if there's any more.
I say no. There is.
The fridge hums. The house leans.
We don't talk about the drinks
or how often we don't.

DAPHNE, WITH THE DOG, WALKS IN ON FRED KISSING VELMA

Yeah, *ruh-roh*'s right! Fred, she is sixteen and you are nineteen! She is a minor! Why is she even on this road trip—I thought you were cousins! The moaning—we thought you were the ghost! I left my whole life for this! Living out of your dirty van, solving stupid crimes about nutjobs in rubber masks—*I am allergic to dogs!* And no one ever pays us for this shit! When have we actually seen a werewolf? You didn't want to commit to me or to college, just wanted to be a hippie to piss off your dad—and this is what you're doing! Making out with your cousin while the dog humps my leg at night?! Where are the keys—give me the keys! Jeepers! What the hell! I wanted to be a dentist! And are you seriously crying right now? Oh grow up, you ascot. Monsters, monsters, ohhhh, they're predictable! Monsters are bad! With bad intentions, animalistic, always wanting something! But people, no. No, no, never that easy. Takes longer to figure out! You listen to me: *humans* are the ones that'll really mess you up. And you'll trust them before they do.

PROPOSALS

Okay, so we'll be vacationing in the Galapagos,
right? And as we're exploring a waterfall,
I get down on one knee and I say,
bby u r the one & only for me
all da other girls mean nothin' 2 me
pls will u marry me
and then you say, *oh myy yes*!
and a tourist comes and takes a snapshot
who turns out to be a magazine editor
and our love story photo lands on the cover
of *National Geography*, er, *Geographic*—

Oh! Yeah, sure, we'll try something else!
Okay, so we'll be on a beach searching for sea glass
to see who can collect the most sea glass, and then,
and as we're counting how many pieces we have,
I say, *hey u forgot this other one*
and you're like, *whereeee* and I'm like,
rightt hereee and I pull out your ring and say,
maarry meee, and then you pretty cry, I ugly cry,
and we drink champagne on the beach and—

Not that one either? Is it the voices?
I can stop with the voices. I'll stop. Sorry.
Okay, so we'll be at Disneyland, right?

And as we're watching that big fireworks show
over Cinderella's hibiscus-pink palace, I—

You don't like Disney? Really? Not even *Tarzan*?
Okay, so we'll be on a night hike instead, so romantic,
under slow-turning constellations, and as we reach
the top of those rose-gold desert cliffs—

Okay, then we'll be at home, cozy winter, video games
together, and then I look into your eyes and—

Okay! Then we're just on a dinner cruise, at sunset,
and I guess our song plays, and I take your hand and—

Okay, it's Fourth of July—

Okay, it's Christmas Day—

Okay, a Busby Berkeley musical—

Okay, a Frank Capra comedy—

Okay, a Jimmy Buffett lyric—

Do you believe in aliens? Have I asked you that?
Then maybe there's a spaceship and it spells out—

asdaklfjlkdsfklhdfskljsflsjasdfklhsafsdfsafskldKFASLDF

Okay.

Have you ever just, like, sat outside in the sun?
And touch a leaf and listen to the birds chirping?
When you see your friends engaged or married,
does their love make you jealous? Or give you hope?
Dating has been difficult. Depends on the day.
So maybe I'll just while away an afternoon instead.

REALLYDRUNK (WHEN IT'S $3.99 MARGS AND YOU HAVE NO SELF-CONTROL;)

I'm a man with my horse on the beach
Wearing my hat, washing my feet

T. S. Eliot was 23 years old when he wrote
"Prufrock," but for my 23rd birthday
I toojk a shot for every guest who arrived
Got to nine before they had to revive me
with frozen bread
I was passed out in a yard!
Couldn't pay me to read something
a 23-year-old wrote
Lives are just differtent

Who else is tired of the whole"
Social media has made us narcissists" thing?
Me. I am. A generation of narcissists!
Like because we take pictures?
Like people in older generations didn't share
what they were doing in their lives?
High-society people used to get their parties
literally published in the papers and stuff
like my brain is constantly manufacturing

or else searching for something to be upset about
So what is the source of this screaming?
Something lying in my childhood?
Biological? I gotta figure it out Maybe.

    YOU ONLY PERCEIVE THIS AS YELLING
    WHEN IN FACT I AM SILENT

You wanna know what I feel?
You know what I wanna feel?
Like the vegatbles in the produce section
getting their li'l rain shower
And they play that thunder sound effect
I know it's to warn folks of the mist
but I like to think the brocollis like it
Nice they do that for the veggies
Maybe God cvould do that for me

Thanks for listening
Had to talk about it

A POEM IN WHICH EVERYONE FINALLY SHUTS THE FUCK UP

!

WE WERE ABSOLUTELY WILD ABOUT EACH OTHER

I think you have an oral fixation. These are the thoughts
that carry me through the night and keep my chest warm.
I got lost somewhere along the way—
nice soft colors making this intimate image.
Feelings of constant timelessness. They tear me in half
when I think of them, stone all the dreams still in flight.
You read my words, I listen to your music,
we dance, we tease, we get dizzy. What does life look like,
with these millions of galaxies and neon halos,   and Pluto,
where they say you can still hear our unkept promises?
An enormous distance, that of our minds.
And I felt so good with you that evening on the seashore,
when you said there are such beautiful loves that justify
all the crazy crimes they do commit.

I am drunk on a Friday night. The Disaronno is gone,
and all I think of is you. I don't want to reach out because
that would not be fair. You are going on dates and living a
life without me. I am working till my feet bleed, and then
beyond that. When memory fails me and I no longer
remember those times, I will think of this storm and
the rain when we'd walk your dog together and talk about
nothing. How my sister is doing in Spain. How your classes
are going. I feel like I must make this journey alone.

Whole novels are like this one night.
Remember when we'd chase the sun in our downtime?
Now I'm making life up as I go. Bring me those who do not
stop to say, "How beautiful," and I will show them our
sunset on the sea at Point Dume. What could be
better than hearing the breaking of the waves, where the
surf sounds loudly, holding you close and watching the sun
go down until everything turns to blue darkness?
We discovered a new world together that night. I never left.
My mistakes, my plans—faded. Only this moment.

Now I'm back in this armchair, and the sun has just set,
and the sky is awash with that late-summer palette
of light pinks and periwinkles.
How I wish I could touch them and bring them to you.
Fold them into a paper boat and have them tell you
how I feel, in your lap on your hardwood floor.
Let them smile at you in their creases and edges;
use my pages as pillows.
And we sleep, and it's like we're there together,
the stars aligned just so.

ARCTIC MONKEYS PLAYED THROUGH A LATE-NIGHT RADIO IN THE RAIN

Standing at the sea,
facing white void.
You beside me,
in your red coat,
and this dog
from the parking lot.
Morning mist. No talk.
We stopped listening
to the news reports.
Out of money,
out of luck,
beyond the ken
of writers who don't write
and stories from our past,
we wait at the future
and walk into the ocean
and the cold
is the first we feel.

FILM SCRATCHES AND DUST

For me, the worst part of you
deactivating your social media
wasn't losing the ability
to slide into your DMs
or to see if you'd viewed my story.
It was realizing I have so few
pictures of you. Just the one,
us together, at an art museum
in August.

When my abuelo died,
I took the photographs of myself
down from his fridge and felt
their edges, the distance,
the year 2005. Twenty later,
and there is so little.

FIRSTS

The first time I had a tamale, I ate the dried corn husk.
The first time I had a poke bowl, I ate the edamame pod.
No one told me otherwise; I was trying something new.
The look of horror on my friends' faces said everything.

The first time I said *orgy*, I pronounced it like *corgi*.
The first time I said *couscous*, I pronounced it *caucus*.
I was drunk at a restaurant with former coworkers and
hoped some baked *caucus* poppers might sober me up.

The first time I had anal sex, I was high out of my mind.
Wasn't thinking or looking at all—just hit the wrong hole.
She stopped me; we stopped. And as soon as I realized
what happened, I apologized profusely. She just laughed.
Then she guided me how.

And my first kiss was while watching a zombie TV show.
I leaned over to my girlfriend in high school, and we kissed,
and she tasted like our apple cider drinks but so much better.
Then zombies attacked, and we had to pause. And resume.
Take us back.

I've made stupid mistakes every day of my life.
To learn things right, you've gotta do 'em twice.

THE RICH, THE ROYALS & THE REST OF US

We've stolen twelve bottles of wine from the resort, our mutual place of employment, and so the twenty of us are at a house nearby after, the sun gone, just our complaints about guests and our managers and our laughs and an obligatory sleeve of Solo cups. It's the last of the wine nights—our ode to Dionysus— and the resort doesn't inventory anyway. We'd know. So it's stories about how staff yelled at Orlando Bloom because he wouldn't put his dog on a leash, or it's Jonah Hill chain-smoking by his van in the parking lot. Here's Gabrielle Union and Dwyane Wade, there's Ewan McGregor and Mary Elizabeth Winstead, Miley Cyrus, Matthew Stafford, Sydney Sweeney. Taylor Lautner was back again today because the rain had flooded his beach house and he wanted a place to watch Netflix. We tell him we voted for him in the 2009 Teen Choice Awards. He says he hopes he won. He's a nice guy. He and his friends here have every amenity imaginable, from vineyard picnics and flatbread-making classes to beachside luaus and outdoor wellness Sundays by the spa. Three hundred and sixty-five days of self-indulgence and bacchanalia, playing with thousand-dollar toys. Not us though.

We are part-time models, freelance screenwriters,
actors in secret, whatever side hustles we can get.
Taking Issa Rae's room service order and stealing this
wine is the closest we'll be to dining like she does.
For now. Champagne wishes and caviar dreams.
And the head of food and beverage is an alcoholic,
a tequila fiend. And the front desk manager wants
to sleep with us—yes, all of us. Ask for a room tour.
How'd we end up here? It was the only place hiring.
Someone ignored all the valet guys' speeding tickets.
Someone's gonna have to ignore all our hangovers
tomorrow—'cause we are long gone and just barely
holding on. Just barely. Tell all our friends back home
that the mayor of Santa Monica says she is *so proud*
to know each of us by first name. Thank you, thank you.
Tell all our friends back home *we wear name tags*.

THE PHONE CALL WITH DAD BEFORE I BLOCKED HIS NUMBER

Women playing softball, women playing shotput,
women, diesel, smell of tires, having conversations
with old people in the Walmart checkout line, his
Taco Bell order, genus *Dendrogaster*, ibuprofen,
his "dumbass" brother, ants, Godzilla's beam attack,
Godzilla's tail-sliding kick attack, the lies he told
my sister and me to fall back into our lives, money
he promised her to help pay for college, the three
thousand dollars I had to find for her, the lies, lies,
so many lies, normalcy she never knew, scattered
pills on the kitchen tiles, kitchen knife, the police,
a sense of normalcy I never got back. Oklahoma.
An apartment where we can visit him, like old times.
Sure. And golf, his dumbass brother. Women again.

RAMONA, CALIFORNIA, FOURTH OF JULY

You wander the land together. Watch frogs
skimming the surface of a small pond,
horned lizards sunning on a stone,
blinking in the heat.
She tells you about summers here,
how her cousins used to race four-wheelers
where the weeds are now.
Family photos on the walls.
Mixed chaparral leans against
open oak woodland,
dusty vineyards, the hush of streams.
Brushstroke memories of a California
before maps, before fences.
Haven't seen a sky like that in years.
"Who is this for?"
What is anything for?
How could there be anything else?
Kid, you are going to the end of the world.
Time doesn't vanish.
It just shifts its shape.
And you, edged with wonder,
are part of it all.

BEERS, BROS, BUNGALOW

(from *Honesty Hour at Surfrider Beach*)

Katie bawled when Julian told her the landlord had scheduled their tiny, nothing-special bungalow for demolition the Tuesday after graduation. She couldn't help it; this was home to her. That was months ago. Now it's T-minus-eighteen hours to leveling, and the plan is for Julian to take her to the airport tomorrow morning before he, too, leaves the state. Rob and Zander ride out together tonight. The others are already gone.

She knows the hardest thing she'll have to do is leave. This was their whisper-thin slice of paradise, a ten-minute drive through the Santa Monica Mountains to the tantalizingly subtle roar of the Pacific. Isn't that what sweet summers are for? Biking and beachcombing beneath flanks of palms. Not packing up the rest of her stuff on what's been the hottest day of the year, both fans running, her body sun-reddened and exhausted from it all.

Julian holds up their engraved beer mugs and asks if Katie is keeping hers.

"Won't fit in my suitcase," she tells him.

He says he'll give it to a friend of his, like, for Christmas or something, and then he wraps the mug in a stretch of paper towels.

There's still work to do outside: the surfboards and longboards; wetsuits drying in the sun; the barbecue grill, tinged with rust from the coastal breeze. Plus the Puerco Canyon road sign they took—"lost in the Woolsey Fire"—that'll have to be left behind.

She loves the bungalow, she loves her boys, and even with all this time to process the move, she is so, so far from ready. She's prepared to spend the rest of the day in protest, watching videos on her laptop while hunched under a blanket. That'll show the world.

But the adult thing to do would be to gather the remaining items and sort through the pile with Rob, Zander, and Julian beside her. So she does.

Five dying houseplants; no forks but plenty of knives; shot glasses from a birthday; tequila; dish soap for handwashing; bruised apples with the stickers still attached.

Rob tosses one of the apples underhand to Julian. He catches it, examines it, asks what you're even supposed to do with the sticker on fruits—"Like, do they really expect me to make my way over to a trash can just for this?"—as he wipes it on the wall.

Zander removes the sticker, rolls it up into a little ball with his thumb and forefinger, argues that a home can't be covered in stickers.

"Upcycle the stickers into a new wallpaper," Katie suggests. "Could be a nice aesthetic."

Rob says you can eat them, that they're made of rice paper and dissolve in your mouth.

Zander says to just put them in your pocket; he has a habit of collecting litter in his pockets anyway if there's no trash bin around.

"So," Katie says, "you guys are just walking around town eating stickers and with pants full of garbage—is that what you're saying?"

"The stickers aren't for you," Rob says. "The stickers have PLU numbers the cashier uses to look up items because a lot of foods, especially apples, look alike and don't all cost the same."

And then it's the four of them deliberating over when's the correct time to empty pocket trash and whether to wash the fruit and how pesticides are just extra flavoring and Julian most certainly has scurvy and GMOs, GMOs, GMOs, GMOs.

Home brew starter kit; rotten left shoe; last week's spinach; lighters; Ohio license plate; wine glasses stolen from the nearby resort; those crushed beer cans on the roof.

Julian says, "Okay, but why do I feel like most people are from Ohio?"

Rob: "Name one person other than Katie."

Zander: "Bro, that's what I was gonna say."

Katie: "You two have lived together for so long, you're practically the same."

Julian: "Like, you ever notice how many songs reference Ohio?"

Zander: "Is Ohio, what, East Coast?"

Rob: "Careful, your Canadian is showing."

Zander: "Says Florida man over here."

Julian: "Canadian? Wake up, people—new Zander lore just dropped."

Katie: "What are you possibly listening to that references Ohio so damn much?"

Zander: "Any of your states I can't immediately point out on a map is stupid."

Katie: "No, if we're talking states, most songs are about California."

Julian: "Okay, but that's obvious. Ohio is so unsuspecting."

Pac-12 and West Coast Conference pennants; Tolkien; yoga mat from house yoga days; hot sauces from that one challenge; disposable masks; volleyball that broke Katie's nose; more tequila; copper-infused pillow.

Zander asks what the hell is a copper-infused pillow.

"It's antibacterial and helps with wrinkles," says Katie. "They put copper in arthritis gloves, and I think it does something for people with joint pain—"

So Julian grabs the pillow and says he wants it, how he will be fully healed from his copper pillow, no more pain, no more arthritis, no more wrinkles, no more bacteria.

Rob, reading from his phone: "The website mentions the pillow will provide benefits to your hair but doesn't elaborate on the nature of these benefits."

Zander wants to know how they infuse the copper, but Julian just chucks the pillow to Katie and declares he'll cut out the middleman and sleep on a copper ore instead, gonna make his whole bed copper.

"I actually sleep in a copper mine myself," she says, hurling it right back to Julian.

"Just glue pennies to the walls and floors," he says, flinging the pillow her way.

"Like those fruit stickers."

"Make sure the pennies were made before 1982."

"Or put a bunch of 1981 pennies in your pillowcase if you're on a budget."

"Which I am."

"Gotta do what you gotta do."

MCAT study guides for general chemistry, behavioral science, biology; clothes everywhere; Rob's missing watch; lots of deodorant; Frank Ocean, BROCKHAMPTON, Childish Gambino album sleeves.

Katie, drenched in sweat, returns from the bathroom in a sports bra. Julian puts a hand to the side of his face, averting his vision. She understands this, along with the kiddy pool he set up for her last week, is his quiet way of showing affection.

"Does anyone wanna explain why everything is so bad today?" she asks.

"The world's top scientists are working tirelessly to unravel this mystery," says Zander.

"Must be because of you," says Julian, now facing her.

"The world demands disorder," says Rob. "Second law of thermodynamics."

"Maybe we camp out behind the bungalow," Julian suggests. "Can't evict us then."

"Dude'll run you over with a steamroller," says Katie.

"Well, I'd be dead, so."

"Can I volunteer to get steamrolled," asks Zander, "or is there a waiting list?"

And so on and so forth.

―――

Hebrew Bible; eucalyptus candle with aloe and essential oils; green grapes; inhaler; letter board that reads, "Give up on your dreams and die. —Levi Ackerman"; parking tickets; poster of surfboarding sloths.

"My debit card keeps getting declined," Julian says, scrolling. "I need to call the number but, y'know, anxiety."

"This," Zander says, "is what happens when you let your kids go on the internet."

Julian picks up the Bible, keeps it. Katie hates to see him hurting. She remembers when the two of them went and blew smoke in a Target and ate their jerky and opened all the umbrellas and lit all the candles. The time they both trekked three miles in a frigid river in shorts to save bank on waders, or when they won the beer die competition together in front of all their friends. Sunset surfs. Tacos in Mexico. She and Julian had their fun, could've maybe been something. But she knows if she brings up deep breathing or therapy, he'll only say it's *his* depression and he can do what he wants with it.

And so, being Julian, he changes the subject to everyone's biggest fears, and then it's all wide-open spaces and the Bermuda Triangle, cicadas and sinkholes, cows—"No, I said *crowds*"—Julian's nose being pushed into his skull, pregnancy, heights, the Kool-Aid Man, bookcases that are also secret doors, observing high-resolution pictures of Jupiter, and jokes aside, being forgotten and being alone.

Rob says he feels like he's always scanning the room for an escape but is never confident he'll be able to leave a situation before it escalates.

Julian smirks, says, "That's because you were in that school shooting."

Rob doesn't reply to that.

———

Plush octopus from Zander's girlfriend; athletic trophies; Japanese whiskey; cardboard with written-out molecular equations; much drinking; college t-shirt from sophomore year.

"My biggest fear," Katie says between pulls of whiskey, then passes it to Julian, "is someone finding out my biggest secret. But I'm telling you all now. Don't judge me; it's grim."

The boys stare at her wide-eyed from the floor.

"Enchant us with your tale," says Julian.

"So I was seven or eight years old, and we lived in the countryside," she tells them. "Our neighbors were, like, a twenty-minute walk away. My mom and I were at their house, and it was getting late, but I was watching *The Lion King 2*. My neighbors offered I stay over to finish watching, and then I could sleep in their daughter's bedroom because she was at her dad's. So I did, and morning came, and I really needed to use the restroom, so I made my way to their bathroom quietly in case I woke them. But when I got to the open bathroom door, the stepdad was turning on the shower, his butt to me. I scuttled back to the daughter's bedroom—he didn't see me. So here I am low-key traumatized but also really needing to go, so what did I think would be a logical solution? I used one of the daughter's t-shirts, then rolled it up and stuffed it all down the side of her bed. Yep. Clearly eight-year-old me thought the problem would disappear. But the next time my mom and I went there, the neighbor mom gave me, like, knowing looks. She didn't ever tell my mom, but yeah, this has haunted me for thirteen years—the time I shat in a Jonas Brothers t-shirt and hid it down the side of some teen girl's bed. I really hope she didn't love that shirt. She probably did. Anyway. The end."

Silence. To Katie, for what seems like eternity.

"What, nothing?" she asks. "I told you all that because I love you."

"Rob, Zander, see that?" says Julian. "She said she loves me, *hyuk-hyuk*."

"Finally," says Zander.

"Appropriate amounts," says Rob.

"We could go to a bar," says Julian, "fake an engagement, get free drinks all night..."

And then the boys can't stop laughing—oh they will not stop their laughing.

And there she is, laughing with them.

———

Melted crayons; dice spread about; beach-brewed IPAs; seashells in a burlap bag; a slew of unifying elements; minifridge with their magnetic poetry on the door.

some women bitter
show their feet through picture
be quick

I will add to door
it looks like it is too short
hell yeah a haiku

reward the smooth peach

stop you mean those sausage s were sun lather ed ?

we was a mess y
friend s together chant worship
but like our lazy ship

please put out my life
I rust in rain
& sleep in shadow
drunk on delirious dreams
let me boil away with time

———

Julian's   Orange   County   Sheriff's   Office   trespass   warning:

"Trespassed from all of Walt Disney World properties to include, but not limited to, Theme Parks, Water Parks, Resorts, and Disney Springs. Conduct not welcome on WDW Property."

He won't elaborate, but Julian sighs and says that that day was the worst anxiety attack he's had in a long time—how his brain went into complete and total shutdown mode and couldn't find anything or remember what anything was called—and he sobbed for eighteen hours straight. Now he says he's so depressed, he no longer cares about talking to anyone. All he wants to do is sleep. He says he doesn't know how to get out of this.

Zander tells the group he literally said this to his doc last week, that Zander feels empty and like a generic cloud of hazy attributes and can't find joy in anything anymore.

Rob says as bad as the past seemed to be when he was living it, he'd gladly trade the present to have it back. That our brains are meat sacks and aren't meant to deal with the modern stress we've invented for ourselves.

"When you haven't been doing super great," Katie says, softly crying while holding one of those shot glasses from earlier, "but haven't been admitting it because it's embarrassing and you think it'll just pass, and you don't want to take the time to talk about it, so it keeps getting worse, and then you're in so deep that you don't want to admit *that* because it'd be obvious you've been lying about being in a good headspace for, like, months. Plural."

The boys all nod in solidarity.

"And it *sucks* not having you guys by my side anymore. I'm so scared it's going to get worse for me out there, and nothing makes me feel otherwise, and honestly, we should be getting some sand between our toes right now, not this, please, anything else but this right now."

"Yes," Rob says, and so does Zander.

Julian says her name.

———

Acoustic guitar; orange sarong; sunglasses; beach towels with clumps of sand still stuck to them; balmy breezes; graduation tassel; an ocean of possibilities, garnished with grapefruit; detritus.

A humpback whale breaches a mile from the shore, and its spray glints at Katie from the car window. She's almost asleep by the warmth of the evening light. Then natural beauty takes ahold of her once more: wild mustards and poppies break to a wide beach, the waves lap a perky honeymoon blue, and that striated sunset sky is so *breathtaking* she forgets she's a person.

"Maybe it's your asthma," Julian says, and she playfully punches his shoulder.

They park, and then Zander and Rob rush into the ocean, tossing seaweed. Katie leans against the car, and she admires the scene. It sneaks up on you, a mode of existing. Camaraderie of this specific, irreverent bent.

"I'm sorry," Julian starts, "that things didn't work out between you and me. There were so many opportunities, and just, it's like..." He smiles incredulously. "It's like the worst thing to happen to us was nothing."

"You don't need to tell me that," she says, a beer in her hand, then swallows the last warm mouthful. "But thank you."

Katie expects Julian next to say some cheesy line about how there's no added weight when you fill your suitcase with memories. Instead, for perhaps the first time since she's known him, he asks how she's doing, and her reaction is one of polite bemusement.

He asks if she'll miss him. She says she'll think about him often. He says to think about someone is not the same as missing them, that when you find yourself losing what you care about, you cycle through everything you have.

Katie thinks this: long from now, she will see Julian in the portion of light coming through a hallway door, holding that engraved beer mug, saved for her all this time. She will recall the bungalow and their lives and know that freedom is only where you begin to scoop clouds with a spoon like whipped cream, and this reality is the same as there, with them, this dream. Once, she spent a year in a dream. This is the feeling that marks where love has touched.

THE FLAVOR OF LIVE FIRE

I wasn't supposed to be on campus when the fire broke out.
I was meant to be crafting screenplays on a yacht, you see,
using my master's degree and talent.
Not back in the college at night and bitter about it.
But I had debt and rent to pay, unemployed for a year
since the Hollywood strikes, and so I got a day job
as an emergency dispatcher for my alma mater.
No one from my graduate program knew; I didn't tell them.
Why would I? I am a writer, and instead, I was spending
my evenings answering medical calls, reports of
sexual assaults, mountain lions, stalkers, psychological
breakdowns, blood on the bathroom floor, panic.
Surrounded by monitors in a windowless room,
I was to calm them all when I couldn't even calm myself.

Then the Santa Ana winds spurred record warmth
and brought floating embers to our dramatic coastline,
and the palms and butterflies and nostalgia caught fire,
and most everything that could have burned did.
Flames flickering in the heavy air, in the midnight dark.
I stationed outside on steps overlooking this special place
of magic by the ocean, once, and I called you.
You answered, at home, brushing your teeth.
You weren't impressed. Tired from your own day,
you said you didn't know how you could help me then.

That fires have happened before and fires will happen again.
Two whole years flashed before my eyes—and the blaze.
I'd put you through enough. You settled on nothing.
I said that's okay, that that's what I needed to hear.

A sobering taste. Our hands together, hands apart.
I removed from my wallet the photograph of us,
edges worn, and left it on those stairs.
I took in the quiet of the ocean and the night's black nothingness
as we drifted across it, carried away by the sea breeze.
That's when I knew for certain.

HATCH GREEN CHILE LAGERS

No one back home planned our ten-year reunion.
So it's just me and Jared from high school
sitting here at this beachside bar in Malibu
that's one thousand, five hundred miles
from our Oklahoma hometown.
A good place to grow up, we say,
but we of course grew up.
Our cars now have California plates,
our wallets with California licenses.
All's left's my Okie accent, on occasion,
when the drink'll get me mighty crossed.
Jared and I've had plenty adventures since
English class, hazy euphoria with new friends.
But you can't play fantasyland forever.

So we're hardworking adults, on our day off,
watching the waves roll in.
A pop song from a decade ago pours out of
the open-air bar while we eat
salsa-capped chorizo burgers and sip
Mexican lagers made with hatch green chiles.
S'got a kick to it, like the kick Jared and I felt
leaving Oklahoma way back when.
The two lone survivors in an apocalypse film,

if we assume to be the protagonists.
It's a bittersweet ending, recalling friends lost.

High school sweethearts Ally and Alan married.
They live in Colorado, maybe, or Pennsylvania.
Mary Faith is in Borneo for her research.
Rowan divorced, gave birth to a baby girl.
And I honestly couldn't tell you what
Hana, Abraham, Nick, anyone else is up to.
We all had a text thread from English class,
but then the years.
As for Bryna, well, there's a different poem.
Are we the last to see this sunset?
Jared has to leave, has to teach in the morning,
but I'll stay a moment more—these beers gone
straight to my head, contemplating infinity,
just a hint of longing on the finish.

SPECTRUM OF BLUES

What if Nemo never made it back to the reef?
What if the anglerfish ate Marlin in the deep—
served with sauces and lime wedges—
or maybe Nemo got caught in the tank's filtration system.
Did that happen to me? Do I find my way?
I must've forgotten, like the blue tang, what's-her-name.
Too much water to see. The ocean gets so big.

I guess I did meet my whale sharks, frogfish, and manatees.
The harbor seal is my brother, giant squid my protector.
They weren't in the movie—but real life never is.
I have lived tank life, and I've seen coral once too.
Snorkeling with cousins in the Caribbean.
An aquamarine shimmer, so close to home,
and Dory, I think these sea turtles are stoned.

WHEN I THINK OF GOD

One Easter, my mother and my aunt hid over a hundred of those colorful plastic eggs for all the cousins to find. Too old to be running around the backyard like that—but there we were: college-aged, collecting candy, and then trading after on the floor together. Everyone won, and they didn't have to hide those eggs. Glad they did.

People will claim God cannot be this or would not be that, and I won't pretend to know what God is not. But when I think of God, I think of my family and loving moments between us. I think of a dog's smile, and not knowing how bumblebees fly but believing that they do. The magic of snowflakes. That planets form, every day. And hallelujah.

THE PETCO GOTH GIRL APOLOGIZES YEARS AFTER

I was avoidant, inconsistent, and unkind,
and none of that was warranted.
I'm truly sorry for...

Is this how people feel reading poems about themselves,
caught off guard by a reaching out that's reaching back?
I saw the woman you were hoping to become then,
in moments. Now she is real—is lively—and here I am,
writing characters still after ghosts I can't shake.
You didn't rewrite the story to make yourself the hero.
You wrote to me to say, "I was hurting, and I hurt you."
A storm I stood in too long. That autumn, we loved
like haunted houses, inviting each other in only to find
more echoes than rooms. We were creatures half-formed;
I name nothing cursed. And I know you write tonight
not to haunt but to bury. To lay it down, bones between.
Ophelia now: not to reopen the crypt but to place
flowers on its steps. You've rebuilt your cathedral;
I pray you're warm inside. I pray you catch your breath.

MY THERAPIST ASKS WHY THIS OBSESSION

Because my summers were swimming at the neighborhood pool
with friends from school and cannonballs and bubble rings.
Flamingo lawn decorations, a prank from Dad's church friends.
When I woke up that late-May morning and saw those hundreds
of poppy-pink birds outside my window, it felt close to magic.
Because he said he'd build me a sorcerer's tower in the backyard.
He left to get supplies and I hope is still out working on it.
Because I read chapter books about humble rodents with all
their stuff tied up in a li'l handkerchief on the end of a long stick.
Because Steinbeck's George had yet to kill Lenny.
Because I had not masturbated, because truth or dare as a kid
just meant sharing who you liked and eating dirt.
Because I'd watched a cartoon about pirates and so was going to
live my life that way: with buried treasure and lapping shorelines
and coconut forests, mermaids, ice cream, sunny dose of yellow,
fruit bats, crabs, geckos. Not long division. Not writing in cursive.
And riding around on my scooter with the cousins, the four of us,
all the same age, really close. And eating that weird waffle cereal,
and pretending to be asleep in the car so Dad would carry me in,
and my dad reading to me some nights before bed, not
realizing he had his problems, not worrying about adult stresses.

Because my folks would divorce in the fall. Trembling limbs, twigs. And because my childhood crush was a girl in the deep end named Sweetwater, and she taught me there's no Cherokee word for *goodbye*, only *until we meet again*. Donadagohvi. That's why.

COMFORT

Lately, it's been poems with nowhere to go,
art without canvases.
I guess I'll write forever, then.
Sunsets, mood sets, big jackets.
Watching the orange of the world
and not being able to put it in your pocket,
like trash,
or to place on a desk at home.
Pastoral music from the kitchen.
Decorations for fall holidays.
I get this from my mother.
There she is, in Cape Cod,
after thirty-three springs in Oklahoma.
In her new coastal town,
it is common for folks to add a
nautical touch,
maritime ephemera, to their homes.
Sea glass and driftwood.
Ship bells to houses.
On quiet, gray days, she'll hear those
handsome ghost ships
faintly chiming,
gently tossing,

as the all-silvered wind blows
and the rustling leaves.
She bundles up every evening for the beach.
What does the rest of the world do?

PRECIOUS

I worry I'll be a dad and not prepared for it.
I wasn't planned—who's to say mine would be?
And I know no dad is ever ready for paternity.
Not in the sense you study for a test,
cram the night before. What would their name be?
If he's a boy, how do I guide him? What is a man?
How do I ensure he doesn't do what I did,
that he's a better person than I was?
And if she's a girl, oh, I know nothing.
How do I help her when she needs it,
ensure she's equipped for this patriarchal world?
I'd hold them so dear. Would do everything I could.
I don't care who the mother is—
I would make sure they are good and cared for
even if it kills me. Especially then.
But—do they come to my apartment on weekends?
Do they swim in the community pool there?
Do I buy them a remote-controlled pirate ship
and cheer as they sail it to the deep end?
Birds and insects trilling. Water splashes.
And when they submerge the ship
to where it no longer whirs, that's okay, darling.
I'm okay. I'm just tired, is all. What am I reading?
A book your mother recommended. I want

to understand her better. Are you hungry?
I barely know what to feed myself. Embarrassing.
I know I at that age wouldn't like what I eat now,
but I would do anything for my child,
anything for you, anything at all.
I remember my father burned the macaroni,
slurring his words, and I called my mother,
and she sped over to pick me up that day.
And don't—you tell me today was the best day
of your entire life. You're only eight years old.
Upbeat music continues on the speakers
and I am so proud. Oh my God, I am so proud.
Eight years old. I didn't think I could do it.
Are you copying me? Don't let me hold you back.

WHO NARRATES THE NARRATOR

When you're asked how you are,
how often do you answer truthfully?

When this book is over,
what will you remember about me?

What's our most important similarity?
What should I let go of, if anything?

What do you think I fear the most?
What advice do I need to hear the most?

What's something they said you'd regret but didn't?
Do you have any movie recommendations?

How would you describe me to a stranger?
Does change always come from anger?

Did I mean for that to rhyme?
What's something that's better the second time?

Will I be back in ten years?
Will you be back in ten years?

Who narrates the narrator?

PRESENTIMENT

This will live in a separate document in case I decide not to include it. If you're reading this, I did. If you're reading this, you know I am annoying and shallow and tired all the time, near insufferable, and there's so much bullshit in the world that I don't know what it is I'm contributing, good or bad. My mother used to call me selfish. It was her only negative view of me, and I know she regrets saying that. I was selfish with my time, preferring solitude so I could work on my writing—and here we are again, a one-way conversation between author and reader. Maybe you'll give this a one-star rating on Goodreads, maybe you'll ask for a refund. Maybe I don't even believe any of this matters, or that anything matters anymore, not me, not the world, not any of it. But if that's the case, then what's the harm in one more poetry book, one more act of self-indulgence, one more cry for help. This is what happened: I became everything I ever wanted. My creative achievements, my many romances, my degrees, my internships, my writing job in Malibu of all places—all of it, granted to me without struggle, without seeking. I knew how fortunate I was, despite the weight of my mother's two divorces, and I also knew my luck would run out. I always knew death was a real thing. My abuelita died when I was six months old, so I never knew her, but I saw how her absence affected my mother. It taught me death happens: no flourish, no drama, just is. So there I was, a fresh twentysomething stumbling in at parties and saying stupid shit like, "Y'know what, when I turn twenty-five, just put me down. I've had my successes, my novels, my lovers. I'll be fine." Immaturity. Annoying, right? But I kept saying it, waiting for someone to take me seriously. I really wanted someone to take me up on that offer. No one did. I was turning twenty-five, and I was so scared of losing everything I'd thought I'd earned that I decided I'll end the story before the story ends me. I'd had my successes, my novels, my lovers, and wrote about it. I wasn't fine. I didn't want to be like biblical Job, whose faith was tested by losing everything. I believed I'd fail if that happened. So one night, alone in Malibu, California, on my bathroom floor between toilet and tub, I drank pesticide. As much as I could. I was desperate. Happens. Lucky for me, a friend answered my phone call, and he drove me to the ER, and they pumped my stomach, gave me charcoal. My friend paid for it with his own credit card so my mother and sister wouldn't find out. I paid him back, of course. And y'know what? I was right. I lost *everything* the year I turned twenty-five, and I lashed out at everyone for it. Annoying, right? How I'll detail my suicide attempt but leave the aftermath vague. Because the particulars are too exhausting to recount: unemployment, living in squalor, seven moves in thirteen months, lies to the woman I loved over the stupidest of things because she didn't love me back the same way, ignoring all my friends out of pride and a better-than-you attitude when I am still that sad, scared little boy I was when I was eight. You don't need the specifics. I'll tell you in person, if it really matters to you. But just know that all that happened two or three years ago now, and two or three years ago it all happened past tense. Now the good news is I don't want to kill myself. This isn't my grave. With a lot of journaling and time to heal, I worked it out. I apologized. I am owning up to the mistakes I've made, taking responsibility, behaving differently. I am leading my child self to a safer place, and we are escaping together. And I don't know what the point of all this was, sharing this information with you. I didn't tell you earlier because I didn't want you to think there was a ticking time bomb to these, to be someone's cause for rumination. I just want you to see me, to know who I am, because these poems are sometimes so grossly melancholic, this misery porn and expressions of grief that have so often been a way for me to drown in the sadness I believe I deserve. The summer is just about over, and soon the fall will settle in, with its colder days, its longer nights, its quiet isolation. But here, as we end this, I want to be straightforward: I will be okay. I'm still not where I want to be, but that's probably a good thing, right? That this journey is still unfolding. Trying to be more generous with my time here. And when I forget, well, I'll read this to myself. And you and I will figure it out from there.

PRESENTIMENT

Poems by

BRYANT A. LONEY

ও☙

LUXAPALILA CREEK
PEPPERNELL
2025

Published by PEPPERNELL
Copyright © 2025 by Bryant A. Loney

All rights reserved. No part of this book may be used or performed without written consent from the author, except for critical articles or reviews. Please do not participate in or promote electronic piracy of copyrighted materials. Please support the author's rights and purchase only authorized editions. Reproduction or use of any part of this book for the training of artificial intelligence technologies or systems is strictly prohibited.

This is a work of creative expression. In honoring both memory and imagination, some names, places, and identifying details have been altered to preserve privacy. Famous figures, where they appear, do so as themselves.

Peppernell is in residence in Fayette, Alabama, by the backing of Luxapalila Creek, a gathering place designed to help writers and artists create and produce. Peppernell books are published and distributed by Verona Booksellers.

Our titles may be purchased in bulk at special quantity discounts for promotional, educational, or business use. Book excerpts can also be created to fit specific needs. For details, write: info@veronabooksellers.com.

ISBN 978-0-9971700-6-1 (trade paperback)
ISBN 978-0-9971700-7-8 (e-book)

Cover and book design by Allison Levens
First Edition: November 2025
10 9 8 7 6 5 4 3 2 1

*And all the lives we ever lived and all the lives
to be are full of trees and changing leaves.*

 —VIRGINIA WOOLF, *To the Lighthouse*

*Well, let it pass, he thought; April is over,
April is over. There are all kinds of love in
the world, but never the same love twice.*

 —F. SCOTT FITZGERALD, "The Sensible Thing"

III. NEW HEART

THE AUTHOR AND THE AUTHOR AT AGE TWENTY-ONE MEET UP AFTER THE FIRST POETRY BOOK

(After Phil Kaye)

— What happened to your glasses? Why do you have a mustache?
— I got corrective eye surgery. When quarantine started and the university sent us home, we got a seven-thousand-dollar refund for housing, and I put that to the surgery. And then I grew out my facial hair as the pandemic went on.
— You look like the Kentucky Fried Chicken man.
— ...
— Or the supporting character in a treasure-hunting movie. Wait, did you say "pandemic"?
— Yeah, just get the vaccines and you'll be fine.
— "Vaccines"?
— And you'll want to wear a mask on airplanes for the rest of your life.
— Weird. So, do we have a girlfriend?
— You'll have a lot of *situationships* but never a girlfriend, no.
— What? What about the Swedish girl in Dublin?
— You two only talk now when it snows. She's a cardiovascular sonographer these days.
— Hmm, so she literally plays with hearts.
— Stop that.

— Where do you live in California? Are we a famous screenwriter?
— You're working on your words. Lots of cool collaborations. You live just outside Los Angeles with your friend and her dog.
— That's cool. Where do I meet her, or when?
— I'll let that be a surprise.
— Oh come on.
— You'll both be wearing Christmas sweaters. She's the most courageous person you know.
— I guess I'll keep an eye out. But who do I date though? Give me names or something.
— It all works out the way it's supposed to.
— That is such an annoying answer. At least tell me who to avoid.
— I shouldn't. Well, avoid Dad, maybe.
— Dad's back?
— Kind of? Not really. No. He'll try to patch things up with broken promises. It all probably isn't worth the trouble. Though one time, he does fly you and your sister out to Oklahoma for a few days at a resort out there, and she and you will spend a good hour sitting in the shallow end of a pool drinking piña coladas and talking about where life's led you both. That's a good memory.
— Nice. Okay. How is she?
— She's doing better. Excited. She's about to graduate from college. You see each other for Christmas each year at Momma's place in Massachusetts. Mom moved for work.
— Oh. Huh. Mom likes it there?
— She really does. She found her people.
— Okay, well, that's seriously great and all, but what, like, tangible advice do you have for me? Isn't that why you're here?

Are we not happy in the future? How do I get happy?

— Don't drink as much, for starters. Especially when you're by yourself.

— I wouldn't. I'm not one of those writers.

— It's expensive. And when you're unemployed, don't spend money like you're not.

— Are we unemployed?!

— Taxes will bite you hard, so watch out. And maybe, I dunno, learn to cook? Food is an area of your life you'll neglect for a long time. In crises, food is your last priority. But it's also the most visible part of you. You need to take care of yourself.

— Fine, fine, fine, fine, fine, but who do I date, or who *should* I date?

— Look, you'll figure it out! Okay? I don't know! Lots of... regrets there. I don't think you're listening to me. It's not easy after this. And I know it wasn't easy then for you either, so.

— ...

— I shut people out and stopped trying to make connections for a while. I hid behind my art. But friends are the best thing for us. Do not resist friendships. And yeah, there will always be heartsore summers. But everything, the good and the bad and the passion and the boredom, will give you your aesthetics and sensitivities. Read *The Artist's Way* by Julia Cameron. Go on hikes, clean the bathroom, make playlists, put up decorations, enjoy the moments when it's 7:38 p.m. and you're about to pack up from hanging out with your friends at the beach all day and then one of them says, "Hey, my house is free! Let's drive there!" I can't guide you to a perfect life, but at least this one's been charted. You will break, mend, soften. You are learning. You still are. That never changes.

— ...
— ...
— But we *are* happy. Right?
— Yes. The best you've felt in years.

CHIMNEY WINE

New Year's Eve wasn't a party this year. No kiss at midnight
with someone I'd been flirting with all evening. Not now.
This is a quieter poem.
This is my sister and me playing the Michael Jackson Wii game
and dancing to "Thriller" in the living room,
trying to beat our high score from over a decade ago.
My mother, tipsy from a single glass of wine,
watches our nonsense from the couch and giggles.
She records us with her phone,
and I look ridiculous in my pajama pants. Earlier today,
we watched the raw sunset together at Mayflower Beach.
I tossed a horseshoe crab shell in my sister's direction,
and she screamed at me the way my mother screams
at the wild turkeys in the road on the drive home after.
The song ends, and we don't beat our score.
We count down the seconds with the New Yorkers on the TV,
gentle in its familiarity, and my mother cries as always—
and this year, I cry too. Why not? Here we are.

THESE TRAILS WE TRAVEL

My new room has my suitcase under the bed and winter clothes
    put away.
My typewriter on the desk, a fresh journal, and a framed
    photograph
of my mother and me, Thanksgiving 1998.
A shelf with the books that survived these many moves:
Into the Wild, *Dandelion Wine*, the collected stories of Raymond
    Carver.
My master's degree in writing for screen and television.
And my laptop, just out of the box, that I can now afford.
LEGO flowers: plum blossom, orchid, bamboo, chrysanthemum.
My own novels, relics to remind me where I've been—
that these trails we travel, we travel with others.
Like the pink envelope, tucked away, from a Ferris wheel girl
    years before.
Like the commemorative pin from the escape room
Amy, Jon, Melissa, and I successfully completed in March,
solving our way through the dark together.
We got appetizers after and congratulated ourselves and laughed.
On the corkboard: a postcard sent from a far-off Thailand
    vacation,
the annual holiday card from Sam and Austin and their cat Sisu,
and a photo-booth strip from the album release party Beth
    invited me to.

A famous singer complimented my sweater, but I didn't know his name.
There's a letter from the high school pen pal who inspired my first novel.
She and her girlfriend just celebrated their three-year anniversary;
we're in the same city now, and maybe we'll someday meet.
Last, a thrifted oil painting of a limousine driver at the beach,
in a folding camping chair beside the limo, watching the waves break blue,
absorbing as much as he can. The sun is so strong and the sky so clear.
Happy to be here. To one more book on the shelf.

DOG PARK PEOPLE

Most days for Maxine's dad are shit, he says,
but time at the dog park makes it a little less shitty.
Or Shih Tzu, I say, a pun that would work better
if Maxine was a Shih Tzu, so everyone just groans.
Maxine's dad is a scientist, and he hates his hours
and hates that Maxine is left by herself all day.
Maxine is a timid big dog on the small dog side,
playing only with Comet while Comet's mom sits
on a nearby bench, on the phone in Russian.
Comet's mom's adult son has mental health issues
and is making life difficult for her—he won't
find a job, won't pay rent, only wants to drink.
She'll be moving out next month to Oxnard.
Maxine and Comet have no idea. And it's a shame,
because Comet's mom is like the social director,
welcoming every new dog and owner to the park,
and Comet, too, has taken on that role with friends.
All the other dogs love to run and play with Comet.
Especially Theodore, my little man, my potato bug,
my beansprout, who comes rain or shine and spends
his time chasing big dogs up and down the fence
and sniffing the grass and investigating the trees
and chasing a tennis ball with me whenever I'm
not chatting with Maxine's dad or Comet's mom.
Theo's mom, my roommate, is stuck at her job.

Her schedule changed, and that's stressed her out,
and so this is how I help. And I really don't mind—
it's healthy for me over here. I talk work woes with
Maxine's dad and am a shoulder for Comet's mom
to cry on while she laments life at age fifty-five.
I share with them my own worries and fears.
Maxine and Comet wrestle by a garbage can, and
Theodore has no calendar, only new smells to find
before it gets too dark to see and we all head home
to eat our dinners, crawl into our beds, rest our eyes.
How nice that these perfect dogs take
their imperfect humans out to socialize.

LUCKY STARS

Yesterday, I ate a popsicle on the porch in the sunlight.
That is to say, I felt like a kid again.
That is to say, I stained my teeth purple.
I am twenty-eight years old,
and I am still fascinated by frogs in nature.
Why they hover within the water like they do.
The sounds they make while jumping in.
I don't know what it is I'm doing,
but I'm learning more about myself each day,
discovering new ways to watch the world.
That car rides can be quiet or with music or calls.
People can dream of you and then not know what to say.
There won't always be sun or even porches,
but I can recollect these moments too.
I'm inspired, I'm here. I'm new.

HOW MANY TIMES HAVE YOU BEEN IN LOVE? AGAIN

Lately, I've been relearning *Minecraft*
with my artist friend Anne,
and I get burgers and beers on the regular
with my musician friend Nolan.
I have catch-up calls with Ali,
and I went to the beach last week with Jared.
My sister got her first tattoo—a bumblebee—
that she's so happy with,
my therapist diagnosed me with
persistent depressive disorder,
and my hardworking mother
gives the best advice
even from the opposite coast.
And there's a little dog I love
I'll occasionally take to the park,
and some evenings past sunset,
it's just the two of us there,
and the sky is summer soft,
and I feel like a cowboy with his horse in the hills
when everything turns to blue darkness.
And years ago before all this,
I dated a girl who I asked to wake me up
if it started snowing outside. She did,

and she ended up doing that
every time it snowed when I was asleep.
She wanted to.
Her remembering to wake me up
was even better than the snowfall.

WRITING IN THE QUIET

I hope my future wife is having a lovely day.
That she got to see this sunshine,
that she's curled up and resting after.
Perhaps she's reading this very book—
unless she's semiliterate. Plot twist!
I'll read to her. I love her face
and the brain behind her face.
Her sandals dangling from one finger.
I swear, she is a shower after playing in the snow.
In her cool cotton robe, she is sexy, sophisticated,
a lighthearted knockout, indie spirit,
a sister to my sister,
summer salve,
mood elevating,
cenote swimming,
roll in the sand,
deepen the time warp,
dinner conversations,
resplendent, inventive,
the orchestra tunes up,
the houselights come down,
surprises all around:
the fairytale castle to my haunted mansion.
Catnaps throughout the property, dazzling.

And maybe she's, I dunno, nice to me.
I haven't had that in a while. Sounds silly to say.
Those Julys,
ones from which I never quite recover,
which I glimpse from now in distant blue.

READY

I am trying again because sometimes love does work.
I am trying again because there was romance in this film
and I want some for myself now.
I am trying again because surely someone likes
golden hour and nice typography
and the sound of an acoustic guitar in a song
as much as I do. I do.
I am trying again because I want to. Not for you or for them
or for my mother or the starry sky—but for me.
I deserve love. Good to say.
So let me love. Allow me to recognize and to receive love,
with open arms and weighted warmth.
How could there be anything else? In all its sweet colors.
These glints of pale light I have processed. I have forgiven
myself, who returns to this page every so often.
I am here with my gentle heart. And if love does not come
tonight, or tomorrow, or tomorrow: I am okay.
Because love will. Let it be so.

MORNING WALKS WITH THEODORE

Theodore is as always sniffing everything—
everything!—
and such good sniffing he's doing.
He wants to smell or kiss or bless every snail shell
on the sidewalk this warm, hopscotch morning.
And greeting each squirrel, rabbit, crow in the park.
Children and sprinklers. Summer's ending.
The last of the incoming ninth graders run their laps,
clutching their abdomens as they slow a moment.
Their coach shouts one more to go, keep going.
The runners wave to Theo as they pass us by.
I don't envy their trek; I did my time years ago.
Theo has no agenda, no clock to check.
I have places I'll need to be, yes, but not just yet.
Theodore dictates our pace,
and our pace is dictated by each rosemary, sage,
lilac, cactus blossom, lavender, orange-yellow rose.
He sniffs them all, and I can't blame him for it,
don't want to blame him for him.
Theodore is not my dog, but he is under my care.
And I walk this dog that is not mine and think of
my former stepfather, impatient, vocal about it.
Once while on a family trip hiking Appalachia
while wearing my mother's gloves—

I'd forgotten mine—
I tossed ever mighty a stick into a lake and accidentally
                              sent a glove with it.
Oh how he yelled.
Oh how disappointed he was with me.
I ran to get it, couldn't reach it, just there.
It's just a glove, my mother told us. It's okay.
But I had ruined the trip; stepdick made sure I knew it,
that I threw it. And so I stopped for a long time
pretending to be mighty. But I've since learned
to be mighty is to observe this big world fully,
to explore and to enjoy and to share in the discoveries.
Theodore is not my dog, but he is under my care.
I never want him to think he's walking too slow when
he stops to smell the roses, and he does smell each one.
Any human concerns I have, Theo helps me to regulate.
Did you see that blue heron fly? We are viewing—
living within!—
the exact same space. Theodore is the best boy:
he is mighty and wondrous and sunny and
oh how he's loved.

CATERPILLAR IN THE GRASS

Caterpillar in the grass
you live
now
you have it
with you
You will see
more than I can
Study you
to change course
than do anything else

FRIDAY WITH CAREFREE CAMPERS

These kids have learned I'm a year older than Google,
so all morning, they're calling me Grandpa Google.
The day is hot. We blow big bubbles and watch
Phineas & Ferb and practice our soccer kicks.
I teach them how to fingerpaint with flower petals.
A boy reads to me a chapter book on dinosaurs.
He's a velociraptor fan. They have feathers now.
My last paycheck missed half the hours I worked.
What's a summer camp to do? Next activities.
They're all beading bracelets and making fairy houses.
Pickleball champs. Fast talkers.
These weird, wild-haired children,
already in a totally different tax bracket than I am—
their moms with mimosas, dads with dark 'n' stormies—
all a Malibu mirage, and I'm waylaid like Odysseus.
A girl has my driver's license, looking it over with
a magnifying glass, and she asks me what "sex" is.
I choke on my grape juice. Other kids starting to stare.
Another counselor saves me: "It just means boy or girl,"
and sure, we'll go with that. Not ready for that chat.
Then her parents arrive, and to her famous father,
I say, "I hope this is okay, but I was a big fan of *Lost*."
He smiles, thanks me, and then comments how
that show must've been two decades ago by this point—
such a long time for him, he tells me.

He and his wife look over at their daughter coloring.
He says they had to leave Hollywood for her
because it's just not the place to raise a kid.
This summer, he says, has been an escape for them.
The girl finishes her drawing, hugs us goodbye.
And I think of all the running around we've done,
all the exhausting days and sore nights after,
setting up those water slides and lugging the hoses,
piggyback rides for these dino-loving children—
and the dino-less world they'll face far from camp
into the years ahead. So, crisscross applesauce,
I tell them to drink their water. And wear sunscreen.
And don't let the balloon touch the ground.

WHAT ARE YOU AFRAID OF

I once dated a woman who would take her deceased boyfriend's
ashes on vacations with her. Scatter in Iceland, Thailand, Mexico.
I thought this strange for the year we were together, but now
I see that's life. That we're all carrying cremated remains of
our past—hers more visible than most. My mother tossed out
the love letters from her second husband, but Christmases,
I'll catch her pining over their Paris pictures.
When our hearts explode, who's there to receive the damage?
When the car makes a noise on the freeway, is it my time,
or do I take it to the shop next Wednesday for repairs?
My roommate's dog chokes once on water, and I lean down
and hold the dog close and tell him he's okay, he's okay.
Outside, I worry I trimmed the rose bushes too short.
Inside, I worry I'll never feel loved again.
I will get hand sanitizer in an open wound at the airport,
will sprain my ankle running through tall grasses with friends,
will stub my toe multiple times on the same household object
and refuse to move said object to a place no longer in my way
until I do. I'm afraid I've done everything in my life incorrectly
until I remember it's the only life I'll ever have. How to spend it.
How to wander through and decide what's for dinner.
There was space debris in the sky last night, and the neighbors
stood out and observed and pointed upward, and their children
asked what that blue wisp was there, why it curled like that.
No one had answers. We all watched together, rare alignment,
enraptured by the beauty of what we cannot understand.

GRADUATION EVE

The evening before my sister graduates from
her college, she, my mother, and I drive to
Orr's Island so that my sister may reminisce.
Bristling firs, granite shores. Water everywhere.
Heartbeat quickens. She tells us of sunrises
and sunsets on this bay, stories of her friends
Luisa, Gwen, Amy, and Ella running around,
how Harriet Beecher Stowe found inspiration
here. Here, where my sister learned sailing her
first week in Maine, ropes in charge of speed.
Classmates capsized, she says, but she didn't.
Almost though—the week she broke up with
her boyfriend from high school and wanted to
leave. Then she camped out here with friends,
and they all swam in their underwear together,
and she felt free. Butterflies on the seafloor.
Academic phrases such as linear temporality,
biologically dimorphic hierarchy, violence as
an ontology of time, others I can't pronounce
(everyone is angry and nothing makes sense).
I don't tell my sister I only talk to one person
from my college days. Not my place. Instead,
I watch a video of her and her roommates, high,
discussing whether they would go back in time
to sail on the *Titanic* if guaranteed to survive

but have to live through the sinking. They yell
the crashing, the terror, survivor's guilt, bringing
something from modern times, like an airhorn.
How this could be a science-fiction short story
where a company sends clients back in time
to live through horrific events in history as an
escalation of thrill seeking. How really this is
just a metaphor for college, I realize, or life,
or reading the poetry collection of a recovering
narrator and all the presentiment it comes with.
Driving back, we pass an overturned ambulance,
abandoned, a reminder there's another story
in the dark as I question my role in this one.
Driving back, my mother plays a CD of a
children's worship album from my childhood,
and I know all the lyrics despite two decades.
How many times did we listen to this? She says
about as many times as we watched *Tarzan*.
Tomorrow, the graduation speaker will claim
love is not intensity but consistency, and my
mother will teach me how to shell a lobster.
The day after, I will move my sister out of
her dorm and then, back in Massachusetts,
she and I will boot up and accidentally set fire
to our PlayStation 3 *Minecraft* town from 2013.
The day after, I will unlock an old cell phone and
rediscover a picture from exactly ten years ago:
the night my sweet girlfriend in high school
put together a book-release party for my
first novel for me and our friends then—
Alan, Ally, Rowan, Mary Faith, Jared,

fifteen others. I'm up on Abraham's shoulders,
mid-laugh, eyes closed. I'd completely forgotten.
And the day after, my sister will receive a
job offer to be a paralegal, my mother will
hike a new trail, and I will fly home to California,
where I will live until I don't, where you will
look to me by way of answering and I will smile.
Wistful music playing, all shouting farewells.
Elementary school, middle school, high school,
bachelor's degree, master's degree, work, after,
the current end. What we find, beginning again.
And will.

ONE LAST THING

And to Bryna, out there, I'm sorry we never
got around to watching *Moonrise Kingdom*.
It's now my favorite of Wes Anderson's,
and I'm so happy you suggested it for us.
I hope you found the chance without me.
I'd tell you all about it—but not today.
What a decade.
Our dogs are long gone,
but they were the best while we had them.
I hope you still think of every corgi as ours.
I hope you don't think of me.

NOTES AND ACKNOWLEDGMENTS

While the cobra bite is the most famous and enduring version of Cleopatra's death, no definitive proof confirms it, and the story persists largely due to its symbolism and drama. Likewise, Fred and Velma are not canonically cousins, and you probably shouldn't eat the stickers on fruits. The quote "All our dreams can come true, if we have the courage to pursue them" is widely attributed to Walt Disney, though there's no verified record of him saying or writing it exactly in that form. The quote "Give up on your dreams and die" is spoken by Levi Ackerman in the 2019 *Attack on Titan* episode "Perfect Game." I was rewatching Isao Takahata's 1991 film *Only Yesterday* when I wrote "Abe," and I wrote "Mr. John James Audubon (1785–1851)" after reading the 2017 graphic novel *Audubon: On the Wings of the World*, written by Fabien Grolleau and illustrated by Jérémie Royer. The nature documentary was the 2022 series *The Green Planet*, produced by BBC Studios, featuring *Antiaris toxicaria*. "Vented Views" is an ekphrastic poem in response to Lincoln Perry's 1989 oil paintings compilation *Maine Moment*, as seen in issue 218 of *The Paris Review* (2016). "Arctic Monkeys Played Through a Late-Night Radio in the Rain" borrows its title from Jacob Darvin's 2018 YouTube video of the same name and is also an ekphrastic poem in response to a screencap from Richard Ayoade's 2010 film *Submarine*. "To Sleep in Spite of Sea" borrows its title from a line in Archibald MacLeish's 1962 poem "Seafarer," as seen in the 2001 anthology *Poems of the Sea*, edited by J. D. McClatchy. "The Fault in Our Expectations" riffs on the title of John Green's 2012 novel *The Fault in Our Stars*, and the poem includes references to several of his young adult novels. "On This, the One-Hundredth Rejection Letter from..." borrows its title structure from Laura Lamb Brown-Lavolie's 2013 poem on the sinking of the *Titanic*. "The Author and the Author at Age Twenty-One..." is after the opening poem to Phil Kaye's 2018 collection *Date & Time*. "The Flavor of Live Fire" refers to the Franklin Fire during the 2024 California wildfire season.

The poems "Marrying My Girlfriend from High School," "Night Windows," and "Land of Fire and Ice" were written during a July 2019 residency at The Writers' Colony at Dairy Hollow in Eureka Springs, Arkansas, made possible by a fellowship from the University of Tulsa. I'm grateful for the space the Colony offered—for the stillness, the porchlight evenings, and the invitation to listen inward.

Thank you to everyone who's been a part of my recent journey: my mother and sister, my family and friends, my roommates and classmates, my coworkers and collaborators, and with special thanks to Anne Perera, Ali Levens, Amy Meador, Tommy Calles, Chrissy Gebert, Jared Gonzales, Nolan Harvel, Landry Hendrick, Betty Yang, Erin Eisenhour, Ethan Veenker, Grant Jenkins, Eliza Dee, Michelle Lovi, everyone at Peppernell, and to you. Reader, you and I shared something here, and isn't that kind of everything? Two people, not in the same room, not even at the same time. Not forever, of course—just long enough to breathe a bit. But this book doesn't end with resolution. It ends with reality, which is: you finish things. Books. Relationships. Muffins. And then what? You rinse your hands, check your phone, and pretend that endings don't feel like being left alone with your thoughts again. I guess that's poetry.

May the words keep flowing.

ABOUT THE AUTHOR

BRYANT ALEXANDER LONEY writes for the page and the screen. *Presentiment* is his second poetry collection; he is also the author of three novels and numerous art and video projects. He received his M.F.A. in screenwriting from Pepperdine University. You can visit him online at www.BryantLoney.com.

www.ingramcontent.com/pod-product-compliance
Lightning Source LLC
Chambersburg PA
CBHW022108090426
42743CB00008B/755